Shooting Stars

Social Fictions Series

Series Editor

Patricia Leavy (*USA*)

VOLUME 35

The titles published in this series are listed at *brill.com/soci*

Shooting Stars

By

Patricia Leavy

BRILL

SENSE

LEIDEN | BOSTON

All chapters in this book have undergone peer review.

Library of Congress Cataloging-in-Publication Data

Names: Leavy, Patricia, 1975- author.
Title: Shooting stars / by Patricia Leavy.
Description: Leiden ; Boston : Brill | Sense, 2020. | Series: Social
  fictions series, 2542-8799 ; volume 35
Identifiers: LCCN 2020025963 (print) | LCCN 2020025964 (ebook) | ISBN
  9789004439344 (Paperback ; acid-free paper) | ISBN 9789004439368
  (Hardback ; acid-free paper) | ISBN 9789004439375 (eBook)
Subjects: LCSH: Self-realization in women--Fiction.
Classification: LCC PS3612.E2198 S56 2020 (print) | LCC PS3612.E2198
  (ebook) | DDC 813/.6--dc23
LC record available at https://lccn.loc.gov/2020025963
LC ebook record available at https://lccn.loc.gov/2020025964

ISSN 2542-8799
ISBN 978-90-04-43934-4 (paperback)
ISBN 978-90-04-43936-8 (hardback)
ISBN 978-90-04-43937-5 (e-book)

PRAISE FOR
SHOOTING STARS

"Leavy has done what she does best: write a story that you won't be able to put down until you finish the final sentence. This book is a shining example of Leavy's talent for writing characters who we root for, and through them, find the inspiration we need to live our lives in the light. *Shooting Stars* is a love story about friendship and real romance, but most importantly, it is a story about learning to love ourselves, the most difficult love of all."

Sandra L. Faulkner, Ph.D., author of *Poetic Inquiry: Craft, Method, and Practice*

"Straightforward storytelling, when done well, can allow the pathos of a tale to flourish fully. *Shooting Stars* offers a prime example – one that grabbed and shook me in a way most novels do not. Patricia Leavy's refreshingly direct narrative voice lulls readers into a sense of cozy familiarity that shatters in an instant, surrounding us with all the horror our minds preserve long after active trauma. I found the story of Tess and Jack uncomfortably resonant and unexpectedly haunting. But the deepest cuts came from Leavy's frankly audacious creation of space for trauma processing and healing as priorities in daily life, rather than the afterthoughts they often become in a world that expects us to smile through pain. If you have survived abuse, *Shooting Stars* will bring you face to face with the long shadow of your own suffering and the fear it instilled. It will make you long for spaces as aspirational as the one Leavy creates in which to face that fear – not only in the moments when it swells, but also in the quiet ones when it breathes in shallow gasps deep within. It is this sense of empathy for self that haunts me most after reading, and that will likely linger in surprising ways."

Alexandra "Xan" Nowakowski, Ph.D., MPH, Florida State University

"*Shooting Stars* is one of the grandest love stories of all time. It contains none of the usual (and silly) formulas – no superhuman hero, no heroine who is impossibly pert while she finds the perfect dress, the perfect shoes, and the best parking spot. Instead, it is a story of love in its many forms: love between couples, among friends, between parents and children, and even love of community and country. It celebrates the power and agency of love to hold its own against the darkest forces of hatred and violence. This is a book that grounds the possibility of hope, love, and healing in our ability, if we will it, to truly see, hear, and accept each other as striving, troubled, imperfect, and ultimately, lovable and loving beings. It will make your heart smile."
Eve Spangler, Ph.D., Boston College

"Unconditional love is curated in pop culture, with whirlwind romances and fairy tale endings. That love has a dark side, though; we are expected to give up ourselves and our values to love blindly. In *Shooting Stars*, Patricia Leavy inspires readers to think about how to love unconditionally with integrity: our lovers, our friends, and even ourselves. While Tess Lee and Jack Miller are healing from past trauma, they learn to love each other in extraordinary ways. Along with their friends, they show us what meaningful love actually looks like, and how it makes us more of who we are, not less. This is a wonderful book that you will relish. Read it on your own, in book clubs, or as supplemental reading in social sciences courses."
Jessica Smartt Gullion, Ph.D., Texas Woman's University

"Leavy offers a creative and compelling representation of love and friendship, gender norms and expectations, and the relational nuances of trauma. This novel is another critical contribution not only to Leavy's extensive oeuvre, but also for authors and artists who seek to use fiction in social research."
Tony E. Adams, Ph.D., Bradley University

"*Shooting Stars* is a beautiful love story – or love stories, as is really the case – for the twenty-first century. In this enticing new novel,

Patricia Leavy introduces a cast of characters with different ethnicities, struggles, sexual orientations, and social classes who come together in peace and harmony through a 'bridge called love.' Tess is a kind of modern superwoman who I can love and admire; she is smart, independent, kind, creative, cares for the arts, humanity, and the earth, turning her troubled past into bright futures for others, loving others for who they are, and letting herself fall deeply and vulnerably in love with Jack. No shrinking violet here. Likewise, Jack is a modern superman. While recovering from his war wounds and emotional losses, he is open to loving Tess, committed to helping her, and deeply supportive of her projects, friendships, and successes. No toxic masculinity here. In fact, while predators lurk in the shadows, in the foreground we bear witness to a cast of good men, those who model what masculinity might look like when grounded in compassion and caring. We need *Shooting Stars* now because it shows that the way between the dark and the light is a 'bridge called love.' For so many of us, perhaps all of us, life is challenging as we learn to live *through* and *with* trauma, grief, and loss. *Shooting Stars* shows us how to thrive through unconditional love. Read this book – it will crack your heart wide open."
Laurel Richardson, Ph.D., author of *Lone Twin*

"*Shooting Stars* is the start of an amazing new turn in the fiction of Patricia Leavy that builds on her previous themes of identity and seeing beyond the surface of people's lives. This novel defies category. It grabs hold of your emotions from the opening line and doesn't let you go, even long after you turn the last page. Leavy writes about abuse in ways that are as devastating as they are realistic, delving into the lifelong impact that childhood trauma has on its victims. Yet this is also a tale of the healing power of love, a love that comes in many forms and finds its way to us through the most surprising people. This is a rare story that demonstrates the ways in which good things come to good people, and how the universe finds balance to the horrors that have the ability to sink us. Her most explicit romance and her most powerful work to date, this is one for every classroom and community

group, taking you on a rollercoaster of emotions but leaving you with a brighter sense of the world and the people who quietly make it better."
U. Melissa Anyiwo, Ph.D., Curry College

"I really loved this book. Leavy's writing is realistic and compassionate. *Shooting Stars* is not just a novel, it's a heartfelt story of love, grief, friendship, and survival that will make you laugh, cry, and most of all, feel truly alive."
J. E. Sumerau, Ph.D., The University of Tampa

"*Shooting Stars* is one of those novels that draws you into its heart and holds you there tightly, as you eagerly move through its contours to discover the fates of characters you have come to deeply care about. Patricia Leavy has once again managed to weave her magic through a story that touches on hugely important themes and critical contemporary issues. At first blush, the book appears to be an enjoyable chick-lit romantic adventure, but this is where Leavy's brilliance comes into play. This is actually a work of accomplished arts-based research, one which is deceptively accessible and deeply theoretical. The proactive reader will note the theory in the story, yet also be pleasured by its potent, aesthetically posed and convincing scenes, elegant and clean writing, and three-dimensional characters. I read it with gusto, called back to it again and again to sit with it and immerse myself in Tess's world. I wanted to know more about her life, her motivations, and her experiences. I found myself eagerly reading to the end, feeling disappointed when I had finished – such is the power of Leavy's writing. This is quite possibly Leavy's best work to date, and I am hungry for more."
Alexandra Lasczik, Ph.D., Southern Cross University

"*Shooting Stars* will touch readers' lives in important ways. An accessible text for scholars in a wide array of academic fields, this love story conveys and explores the power of interaction and relationship as they shape and reshape characters, relational bonds, and love. Quite

simply, this latest offering from Patricia Leavy is a labor of love. It is well worth reading."
Keith Berry, Ph.D., University of South Florida

"A few years ago, I stumbled upon Patricia Leavy's 'An Open Letter to the Facebook Friend Who Thinks My Life is Perfect.' I was so drawn in by the writing of the author who wrote this impactful piece, that although it was out of character, I reached out to Patricia to learn more about her writing. Three years later, my uncharacteristic act has gifted me with access to several of her works to utilize with my students in the classroom setting. They, too, have fallen in love with Dr. Leavy's writing. It is hard to imagine, having read so much of her work for both pleasure and academic guidance, that the standard Leavy has set for social fiction could reach any higher, but *Shooting Stars* has done just that. This healing story has left an indelible mark on my soul. I am thrilled to finally have a resource that will serve both as a learning tool for students and a healing tool for anyone who has experienced trauma."
Renita M. Davis, LICSW, PIP, Troy University

Selected Fiction from Patricia Leavy

Candy Floss Collection

Film

Low-Fat Love Stories
By Patricia Leavy and Victoria Scotti

Blue

American Circumstance: Anniversary Edition

Low-Fat Love: Expanded Anniversary Edition

For more information, visit the author's website
www.patricialeavy.com

For Mark,
and all those who help us heal
and walk the bridge from darkness to light

CONTENTS

ACKNOWLEDGEMENTS

Thank you to everyone at Brill | Sense for supporting this book and my growth as an author. Special thanks to John Bennett, Marti Huetink, Jolanda Karada, Els van Egmond, Dan Carney, Caroline van Erp, Evelien van der Veer, and Robert van Gameren. Thank you to the editorial advisory board members of the *Social Fictions* series for your generosity, and to the early reviewers for your generous endorsements. Heartfelt thanks to Shalen Lowell, the world's best assistant, spiritual bodyguard, and friend. Thank you to Clear Voice Editing for the always phenomenal copyediting services. To my social media community and colleagues, thank you boundlessly for your support. My deep gratitude to my friends, especially Tony Adams, Vanessa Alssid, Melissa Anyiwo, Keith Berry, Celine Boyle, Renita Davis, Pamela DeSantis, Sandra Faulkner, Ally Field, Robert Charles Gompers, Joel Gopen, Alexandra Lasczik, Linda Leavy, Laurel Richardson, Xan Nowakowski, Mr. Barry Mark Shuman, Jessica Smartt Gullion, Eve Spangler, and J. E. Sumerau. My love to my parents. Bob Leavy, you're a wonderful father and I adore you. Madeline Leavy-Rosen, you are my light and my heart. Mark Robins, you're the best spouse in the world. Thank you for all that words cannot capture. I love you, always. To those healing from trauma, I see you. And to those who walk alongside, I salute you. This book is for you.

CHAPTER 1

"How's your son doing in school?" Tess asked the bartender.

"Really well. He especially loves the history course he's taking."

A man came in and sat two stools down from Tess. They looked at each other and smiled in acknowledgment.

"Hey, Jack. The usual?" the bartender asked.

Jack nodded. "Please."

Tess continued chatting with the bartender as he served Jack a bottle of beer. "The humanities are so important. It's a shame they're undervalued," she said.

"You're the expert," the bartender replied.

Just then, a different man sidled up to Tess. "You have the most beautiful brown eyes," he said.

"Do I?" she asked.

"And the way your hair flows all the way down your back. You know what they say about dirty blondes?"

"I don't think you should finish that sentence," Tess said.

"I've been watching you. Can I buy you a drink?" he asked.

"No, thank you," she replied.

"Come on, just one drink. I'm a nice guy."

"No, thank you," she said, turning away.

The "nice guy" opened his mouth to protest, but Jack stood up with an imposing air and said, "The lady said no."

The man huffed and walked away.

"Thank you," Tess said.

"Don't mention it. I did feel a little sorry for him, though. You are beautiful and I can't blame him for taking a shot."

Tess smiled and pulled out the stool next to her. "Please, scooch over. Let me buy your drink."

He smiled and took the seat next to her. "My name is Tess Lee," she said.

"Jack Miller," he replied. "But it's on me. Yours looks nearly empty. What are you having?"

"Sparkling water. I don't drink. It's just a personal choice," she replied.

"Another sparkling water for my new friend," Jack said to the bartender. "So, Tess, what brings you here by yourself?"

"I was supposed to meet my best friend, Omar, but he had a last-minute emergency. His partner, Clay, was pulled over tonight and it became an incident."

"What was he pulled over for?" Jack asked.

"Being Black," Tess replied. "Clay is a surgeon and was on his way home from the hospital. He was pulled over for no reason and harassed. It's happened to him before. Once, he was on his way to an emergency at the hospital, and he was detained even after he showed his hospital ID. It's egregious. Anyway, I told Omar to stay home with him. They need time together to process and decompress. I was already in a cab on my way here, so I decided to come anyway. I moved to DC from LA about six months ago and I don't have that much of a life yet, I suppose. And you?"

"My friends ditched me. We usually get together on Friday nights at a different bar, but they all had to stay late at work. This place is right down the block from my apartment."

"So, what do you do?" she asked.

"I'm a federal agent with the Bureau, working in counterterrorism. I joined the military right out of high school, Special Forces. I was in the field, often deep undercover, until about a year ago, when I took a desk job as the head of my division."

"Wow, you're like the real-life Jack Bauer. You even look a little like him, with that whole rugged, handsome, hero thing you have going on," she said.

He blushed. "I promise you I'm no Jack Bauer, even on my best day. People thought that character was so tragic, but the real tragedy is that Jack Bauer doesn't exist and you're stuck with guys like me."

She smiled. "What made you choose that line of work?"

"My father was in the military and then became a firefighter. The idea of service always seemed important. I wanted to serve my country, to protect people. It's hard to explain, but when I see someone innocent being threatened, I'm willing to do whatever is necessary to protect them. I know it sounds cliché, but I feel like it's my purpose in life."

"That's noble," she said.

He shook his head. "The lived reality often isn't. When you spend most of your life in the abyss, it gets pretty dark."

"A residue remains, right?" she asked.

He looked at her intently, a little surprised. "Yes, exactly."

"I understand. You convince yourself it's all been for something that matters more than you do, that whatever part of yourself you sacrificed was worth it, because it simply has to be."

He looked at her as if she had read his innermost thoughts. "Yes," he said softly. "Tell me, what do you do?"

"I'm a novelist."

"What are your books about?" he asked.

"That's a hard question to answer. I guess I wanted to write about everything: what it means to live a life, why it's so hard, and how it could be easier. Perhaps my goals were too lofty, and in that respect, each book fails more spectacularly than the one before."

The bartender smirked.

Tess wistfully said, "Maybe reality can never live up to our dreams."

They continued talking, completely engrossed with one another. Two hours later, Jack said, "I live nearby. Do you want to come over for a cup of coffee?"

Tess looked him straight in his warm, blue eyes. "I'd love to."

Jack threw some money down on the bar to cover both tabs. The bartender said, "Ms. Lee, are you sure you're all right? I can call you a cab."

"You're very kind, but I'm fine. Thank you."

Jack opened the door and held it for Tess. "Do you know the bartender?"

"Just met him tonight," she replied.

"Down this way," Jack said, taking her hand as if it were completely natural. They approached a homeless man on the corner asking for money. Tess walked right up to him, pulled a twenty dollar bill from her pocket, and handed it to him. She held his hand as she passed the bill, looked in his eyes, and said, "Be well."

As they walked away, Jack said, "That was really sweet, but you should be more careful."

"I trust my instincts," she replied.

When they arrived at Jack's small apartment, he took her coat. She glanced around and noticed the walls were completely bare. "How long have you lived here?" she asked.

"About nine years," he replied. "Can I get you some coffee or something else to drink?"

She shook her head and meandered over to his bedroom. He followed. He took the back of her head in his hand and started to kiss her, gently and with increasing passion. He pulled off his shirt and they continued kissing. He pulled back to look at her and she noticed the scars on his body: two on his right shoulder, another on his abdomen, and smaller marks along his upper arms. When he noticed her looking, he turned around to lower the light, revealing the gashes across his back. She brushed her fingers along the deep marks. "I'm sorry," he said. "War wounds. A couple of gunshots. Some other stuff from when I was in the Gulf. I know it's gruesome."

"It's wonderful," she whispered.

"What?" he said.

"I'm sorry, I didn't mean it that way. It's just that I've never seen anyone whose outsides match my insides."

He looked at her sympathetically.

"I was abused when I was little. My grandfather and my uncle. It started when I was eight. No one can see my wounds, but they're there."

He stood still, looking at her.

"I'm so sorry. I've never shared that with any man I've been with in my entire life, and I just met you. That has to be the least sexy thing ever. I'll leave," she stammered, trying to walk past him.

He took her hand and pulled her back toward him. He cupped her face in his hands, gently caressed her cheeks, and kissed her. They made love with their eyes locked on to each other. Afterward, he held her in his arms and said, "That was so special. Spend the day with me tomorrow."

"Okay," she replied, and they fell asleep, their limbs entangled.

***

The next morning, Tess awoke to find a note on the pillow beside her that read, "Went to get breakfast. There's an extra toothbrush on the bathroom counter. Back soon."

She brushed her teeth, and by the time she was done, Jack had returned.

"Hey, sweetheart," he said, as if they had known each other for years. He pecked her on the cheek. "I didn't know what you like so I got bagels, muffins, and a fruit salad. Do you want coffee?"

"Yes, please."

He poured two mugs of coffee and they sat down at the small table. "What kind of food do you like, anyway?" he asked.

"I'm a vegetarian. I don't believe in hurting living beings."

Jack looked down.

"Innocent beings," she said.

He smiled. "I guess that's why you're so tiny."

She started picking at the fruit salad. Jack noticed that she was moving it around with her fork, almost like she was counting. He looked at her quizzically.

"I'm weird with food. I don't eat that much. It's kind of a control thing," She paused, keeping her eyes on her breakfast. "I have problems."

He reached across the table and put his hand on hers. "That's okay. We all have problems. They make us human."

They spent the day together, talking, watching TV, and walking around his neighborhood. They got Chinese takeout for dinner and made love twice more. Sunday morning, Tess realized she'd missed a dozen calls and text messages from Omar. She called him while Jack was making coffee.

"I promise, I'm fine. I'm sorry I worried you. I met someone. His name is Jack. He's special... Well, if he is holding me hostage, don't pay the ransom. I want to stay... I'll text you all about it... Okay, love you, too. Bye."

"He was worried about you?" Jack asked.

"He's been looking out for me for a long time. We talk every day, but I guess I was too preoccupied yesterday," she said, slipping her hands around his waist.

"Sounds like a good friend," Jack said.

"He's more than that; he's my family. He moved here a year ago and convinced me to leave LA so we could be in the same city. But enough about him. Right now, I'm only interested in you. Come here," she said, walking backward toward his bedroom. Just as he was about to touch her, she grabbed a pillow and walloped him.

"Oh, you're in trouble now," he said, darting for a pillow. They tumbled onto the bed, laughing.

They spent the rest of the day lounging around Jack's apartment, reading the Sunday newspaper, and sharing stories. That night before they went to sleep, Jack said, "I don't want the weekend to end. Do you have to work tomorrow?"

"Well, I do work for myself. Can you take the day off?"

"I once took two weeks off, but other than that, I've never taken a single day off in over twenty years. So yeah, I think I'm due for a personal day."

***

The next day, Tess and Jack went for a walk and ended up at a local park. They sat on a bench, huddled together in the chilly, late autumn weather. Suddenly, a little boy ran over and tugged at Tess's coat sleeve.

"Do you have superpowers?" he asked. "My dad says you do."

"Excuse me?" she said.

His father came running over. "I'm so sorry if he was bothering you, Ms. Lee."

"Not at all," she replied with a gracious smile.

"I'm a librarian. I want to thank you for everything you've done," he said.

"My pleasure," she replied. "Thank you for what *you* do."

The little boy tugged at her sleeve again. "Well? Do you have superpowers?"

His father laughed. Tess looked at the boy and lowered her voice conspiratorially. "I'll tell you a secret. Everyone has superpowers, they just don't know it."

"Even me?" he asked.

"Especially you," she replied.

Jack smiled.

The man took his son's hand. "I think we've bothered these people enough. Thank you again, Ms. Lee," he said, leading his son down the path.

Jack looked at Tess. "That was so sweet, what you said to that boy."

She leaned over and kissed him.

"What was the deal with his father? It seemed like he knew you."

"I did some volunteer work for the library a few months ago," she replied.

A few little girls came skipping past them, drawing their attention.

"It's starting to get cold. You want to go to a movie?" Jack asked.

"Sure."

After the movie, they went to a neighborhood Italian restaurant for dinner. The maître d' greeted Tess like an old friend. "Ms. Lee, such a pleasure. We have our best table for you."

"I guess you've been here before," Jack said as he pulled out her chair.

"Jack, listen to the music," she said.

"Sinatra – the best."

"Let's dance," she said.

He looked around. "I don't think they have dancing here."

"But I love to dance," she said.

He stood up, took her hands, and they danced by the table. "You know, I'm not much of a dancer, but I promise to dance to as many slow songs as you want."

7

"Maybe someday we'll have a special song," she said, nuzzling into his chest.

Later, when they got back to Jack's apartment, he led her to the couch with a slightly serious look. "I need to tell you something."

"What is it?" she asked.

"You've seen the scars on my body, but there's another side of it. Tess, I've done things – things that may be unimaginable to someone as sweet as you, things I had to do to protect innocent people." He proceeded to tell her every act of violence he had ever committed, his life laid bare at her feet. The list was long, the death count high.

When he finished, she said, "You did what you had to do for your job. I don't understand why you're telling me this."

"Because I'm in love with you. I'm completely madly in love with you and I've never felt that way about anyone. With the things I've done, I don't expect that you could ever feel that way about me, but I needed you to know who I am." He looked down.

She stroked his cheek. "Jack, I'm in love with you, too. I spent our first night together memorizing your face: every line, edge, ridge, pore. I knew you were the best thing that would ever happen to me and I was afraid the memory would have to last a lifetime."

"I feel like the luckiest man in the world."

"Jack, let's not worry about all of the details of our pasts. I want to leave the pain behind and just love each other now."

He smiled. "Okay, but maybe I should at least know how old you are and when your birthday is."

"Thirty-eight, and I never cared for holidays, including birthdays."

"Got it. Forty-two and you're the only present I'll ever need." She smiled.

"Let's go to bed," he said.

The next morning, Jack went to work and Tess went home. At the end of the day, they met at his apartment. "I have something for you," he said, holding out a velvet box. "I was passing an antique store and saw it in the window."

She opened the box to reveal a gold heart locket. She beamed and her eyes filled with tears. "Jack, it's the best present I've ever received," she said, putting it around her neck. "I'll wear it every day."

"You have my heart, Tess. My whole heart, forever."

"Promise me something. Don't ever buy me another present again. Nothing could ever be better than this."

"I'm hoping life is long. That's a lot of birthdays, holidays, Tuesdays," he said.

"Flowers. You can always get me flowers if you want to," she replied.

"Which ones are your favorite?"

"White hydrangeas. I never buy them for myself," she said.

They kissed, and then Jack got up and turned some music on. He reached for her hand. "Let's dance."

The second song that played was "All of Me." Two lines into the song, Jack said, "This is our song, I just know it is. Okay, baby?"

She nodded and rested her head on his chest.

They continued to work each day and spend each night together. Thursday night, Tess made eggplant parmesan, which she brought over to share with Jack. While they were eating, he said, "My friends and I go to this place called Shelby's Bar every Friday night. I told them all about you and they really want to meet you. Will you meet us there?"

"Of course," she said. "Tell me about them."

"Joe is in his mid-fifties. We've worked together for about fifteen years. He's a class act. Bobby is young, twenty-nine, and the nicest, most laid-back guy. He joined the Bureau three years ago, but I feel like I've known him forever. His girlfriend, Gina, is an elementary school art teacher. You'll like her."

"Sounds great. What do you think about bringing an overnight bag and staying the night at my place after we hang out with your friends? It's about time you see it. Omar and Clay are coming over for brunch on Saturday and I'm dying for you to meet each other. Will you?"

"Absolutely," he replied.

"Jack, you know how people always talk about all the things they want to do or see in their lifetime? They don't even mention being happy because I suppose they think that's just a given."

"Yeah."

"Happiness has never been a given for me. I guess I pursued other things," she said.

"Me too," he replied.

"But I'm so happy now, with you."

"I love you so much, Tess."

"I love you, too."

CHAPTER 2

"Joe, I'm completely in love with her," Jack said, taking a swig from his beer.

"I honestly never thought I'd see the day," Joe replied.

"I told her how I felt and it didn't scare her. She said she loves me too, and I know she means it."

"I can't wait to meet her," Joe replied.

"She's sweet, smart, and so beautiful. There's a gentleness about her. From the first night we met, there was something indescribable between us. It's like my heart just cracked open," Jack said. He took a sip of his beer. "All I want to do is spend time with her."

Joe smiled.

"She'll like this place, especially when the music comes on later. She loves to dance."

His mouth fell open. "You dance?" Joe asked in disbelief.

"The slow songs, as many as she wants."

"Wow, you've fallen hard."

Jack smiled. "There she is," he said when Tess walked through the door.

They both stood up as Tess approached the table.

"Hi, sweetheart," Jack said, kissing her. "This is my friend, Joe. Joe, this is…"

"Tess Lee," he interrupted, staring in awe. "It's a real honor to meet you."

Jack looked at him curiously.

"Nice to meet you, too," she said.

"I didn't realize… Jack never mentioned," he stuttered. "Well, he never said your last name."

Tess smiled.

"Uh, please, let's sit," Joe said.

They all sat down, Jack and Tess in the booth, and Joe in one of the surrounding chairs.

"This place is cool," Tess said, looking around. "Is this for me?"

"Yes, I ordered you a sparkling water," Jack said.

"Thank you."

"Tess, this is truly an honor. Your writing is wonderful. I've read many of your books," Joe said.

"That's very kind," Tess replied.

Bobby was the next to arrive. He dropped into a chair opposite Jack, extended his hand, and said, "You must be Tess. Great to meet you." Then he signaled for the waitress to bring him a beer. "Gina should be here any minute. She had parent teacher conferences this week." He grabbed a fistful of pretzels from the bowl and started munching on them. "You look really familiar," he said to Tess. "You must have one of those faces."

Tess smiled.

Bobby continued, "Everyone needs to be extra nice to Gina tonight. Yesterday this one jerk said he wished his kids spent more time in math and less in her art class. You can imagine how she felt. God only knows what happened in those meetings today. Tess, you must relate. Jack said you're a writer."

Tess smiled widely.

"Bobby," Joe said softly. "Actually, Tess is…"

But before he could finish, Gina flitted over. Bobby stood up and gave her a peck. "Hey, babe. I just got here a minute ago. This is Tess."

Gina's jaw dropped. She patted Bobby on the chest as she fell into her chair. "Bobby, this is Tess Lee. *Tess Lee.*"

Jack looked at Tess, a little lost.

"I'm sorry," Gina said, staring straight at Tess. "I'm just in shock. I love your work so much. This is just incredible."

"Well it's very nice to meet you, Gina. You're very kind," Tess replied.

Gina turned to Bobby, "Is this really happening?"

Tess looked down and put her hand on Jack's leg. Her cell phone rang, so she retrieved it from her handbag and looked at the screen to see who was calling. "I don't mean to be rude, but this is an international call I've been missing all week. Please excuse me while I step outside for a minute."

As soon as Tess was out the front door, Gina hit Bobby's arm. "Why didn't you tell me? She must think I'm a moron, the way I was gushing."

"What are you talking about?" he asked, pretzels spilling from his hand.

"What's going on?" Jack asked.

"Jack, Tess is one of the most successful authors in the world," Joe said.

"And my personal hero," Gina added. "Bobby, her books are on my nightstand. You've seen her picture a thousand times. Not to mention she's been interviewed on all of the late night and morning talk shows."

Bobby shrugged.

"You really don't know who she is?" Joe asked.

"I guess I don't read a lot," Jack replied.

"They make movies out of her books, too. You probably know who she is, but you just don't realize it," Joe said.

Bobby picked up another handful of pretzels. "Gee, Jack. I would've figured you would have done a full background check on any girl you brought home. You didn't even Google her?"

Jack looked to Joe for an explanation. "She's worth over five hundred million dollars, Jack."

"I had no idea," he mumbled, shaking his head.

"It's a remarkable story," Joe continued. "She published her first novel right out of college. It was a start-up publishing house and they accepted unsolicited submissions. She didn't even have an agent. Her book became an international bestseller and won a slew of awards. The next book hadn't been contracted to anyone yet, so publishers had a bidding war trying to get their hands on it. She had so much power and used it in the cleverest way. Instead of taking a seven-figure advance from one of the big publishers, she agreed to stay with her small indie publisher under special conditions. Bottom line, they would distribute the English-language version of her books, but she owned all the rights: licensing, translations, entertainment, the works.

It was an unprecedented deal that allowed her to build an empire. She releases a novel every year and has a famous collection of essays. To this day, she doesn't work with an agent, so she's never had to give a cut to anyone and she controls how her work is adapted and distributed around the world."

"How do you know all of this?" Jack asked in disbelief.

"I read about it in *Time Magazine* and *Newsweek*."

"She gives most of what she earns to charity," Gina added.

"We were in the park the other day and this man thanked her for something she had done for a library," Jack said. He paused and shook his head. "She said she had done some volunteer work."

"She's donated millions to public libraries and raised tens of millions more. I read that she's had a grueling book tour schedule for most of her career, and that while she's on the road, she gives public talks promoting literacy and advocating for the arts," Joe said.

Gina picked up Bobby's beer and guzzled it. "Wowza. Okay, I can breathe now. Yeah, Joe's right. Every librarian, humanities teacher, art teacher, and aspiring writer I know idolizes her, not to mention women in the business world. She's a legend."

Jack sat for a moment, trying to process everything. He noticed Tess come through the front door. "Excuse me," he said to his friends, getting up and crossing the bar to meet her.

"I'm sorry," she said. "I hope your friends don't think I'm rude. I've turned that stupid phone off for the rest of the night."

He put his hands on her shoulders. He could barely look at her. "I'm so embarrassed."

"Why? What happened?" she asked.

He looked down, as if searching for the words. "I didn't know who you are," he muttered.

"I don't understand. You know me better than anyone."

He glanced back toward their table.

"Ah. That isn't who I am, it's what I do. Sometimes it confuses people." Her expression took on a glint of sadness. "You're not confused, are you?"

He looked into her eyes and brushed the hair out of her face. "No baby, I'm not confused."

***

"I love these old brownstones," Jack said. "Which floor are you on?"

"The whole thing is mine. It was converted into one giant home years ago. I was lucky to snag it when I moved to DC. Your friends are great. They're so much fun," Tess said, as she unlocked the door.

"They loved you, too. I think you made Gina so comfortable by the end of the night that she actually started to see you as a real person," Jack replied.

Tess giggled. "Come on in," she said, as they walked upstairs and into the large, open-concept kitchen and living room. "Let me take your jacket." He handed her his jacket and she hung it in an organized closet. "Your friends were really talking you up. They think the world of you. Do you know how many times they told me you're the most honorable, loyal person they know?"

"I guess they thought I needed help," he joked.

"Well, you don't," she said, wrapping her arms around him.

He caressed her shoulders. "This place is gorgeous."

"It's too big for me, but that's what I get for buying it sight unseen. Omar picked it out. The dining room is around the corner, my bedroom is down that way, the second floor has guest rooms, laundry, and a gym, and the top floor has been converted into an obscenely massive library and office. You can poke around tomorrow."

"It looks like you've lived here for years," Jack said, admiring the art on the walls.

"When Omar convinced me to move here, he promised to have the house set up so it would feel lived in and I wouldn't lose writing time. He's a man of his word."

"But what about the mantel?" Jack asked. "It's bare. It would be a nice spot for photos."

"I don't really have any photos," she said.

"Hey," he said. He pulled her toward him and wrapped his arms around her waist. "Show me your bedroom."

***

When Jack woke up the next morning, Tess was already showered and ready for the day. She was slipping a bracelet on, and when she noticed he was awake, she sat down beside him on the bed. "Good morning, baby."

"Good morning, sweetheart," he said. "What time is it?"

"After nine. You were tired. Omar and Clay will be here at noon. I need to run to the bakery to pick up the dessert I ordered, and then I'll get the frittata ready."

He scooched over and lifted the blanket. "Come spend a few minutes with me first. I'll go to the bakery, so you have time."

She crinkled her face. "Well, I guess if you'll do that, we can be cozy for a few minutes."

She crawled into bed and leaned against him.

"Tell me about Omar and Clay. You made a hell of a first impression on my friends; now I need to do my part with yours."

"They'll love you because I love you. Omar is my everything, well, until you. He's my best friend and my only family. We've been a team since college. I couldn't survive without him."

"Where's he from? What does he do?"

"He was raised in London, went to college in New York with me, and then moved to Chicago for graduate school. He's a clinical psychologist, but by the time he graduated, I desperately needed someone smart who I could trust to run my licensing business, and he's such a good friend that he agreed to help me out. He changed his whole life for me. Who does that? I don't know how I got so lucky."

"That's incredible," Jack said.

"He still does his own work part time. He moved here about a year ago when he got a big research grant from the National Institute of Health. He's part of a team that is studying how art impacts our emotional intelligence and well-being. It's amazing work."

"And Clay?" Jack asked.

"They've been together about four years, and I absolutely adore him too. He's a trauma surgeon and the nicest man you could ever meet. He's been very generous. Omar traveled with me when he could and he spent loads of time at my place in LA. Clay has always respected our relationship. It's easier now that we're all in the same city. It's why I agreed to move here. Omar had done so much for me, and I felt it was my turn. You'll love them."

"Well, I'd better hop in the shower because I don't think we want them to find us like this."

Tess giggled. "I'll go make coffee."

***

Omar and Clay arrived at noon.

"Hello, Butterfly," Omar said, kissing the top of her head.

"These are for you," Clay said, handing her a bouquet of pink flowers.

"They're beautiful, thank you. This is Jack," she said, touching his chest, "And this is Omar and his better half, Clay."

Omar shot her the side eye.

"Nice to meet you," they all said, shaking hands.

"Let me take your jackets. Brunch is in the living room, please go sit," Tess said.

Jack sat on the couch, and Omar and Clay took the chairs. "What can I get everyone to drink?" Tess asked.

"Well it's brunch, Butterfly. There bloody hell had better be cocktails," Omar joked.

"Of course. What would you like? A mimosa?"

Omar nodded.

"Make it two, please," Clay said.

"When in Rome," Jack said.

Tess went to retrieve the drinks while the men chatted.

"Tess has told me a lot about you," Jack said.

"Likewise," Omar replied. "In the twenty years I've known her, she's hardly shown any interest in the would-be suitors that have tried to catch her eye. Now I'm getting a dozen texts a day about you. I must say, I was dying to meet you."

Jack blushed. "Tess is quite a woman." He glanced over to the kitchen. "I'm still waiting to wake up from this dream, because she's perfect."

"Oh, well I'd be happy to tell you about her many flaws. Let the nightmare begin," Omar jested.

"I heard that," Tess called, carrying four champagne flutes on a tray, three with mimosas and one sparkling water.

"I'm impressed, Butterfly. If this writing thing doesn't work out, maybe we can get you a job at a saloon."

"I do love a good peasant skirt," she said, knuckling the top of his head and tussling his hair.

"Now I'm going to have bad hair all day," he complained.

"Serves you right," she said, plopping down beside Jack.

"We were just getting ready to tell Jack about your flaws," Omar said. "Where shall we begin?"

"Clay, was I this terrible when I first met you?" Tess asked.

"No, you weren't. You were the epitome of grace and kindness," Clay replied.

"I'm just teasing," Omar said, smiling at Tess. He turned his attention to Jack. "Truly, we're so happy to meet you."

"Tess said that you two have been friends since college, but she didn't mention how you met," Jack replied.

"Everyone, please take some food," Tess said.

They all helped themselves to the artichoke and tomato frittata and green bean salad.

"Tess and I met on our first day of college. It was orientation day, where they put you in groups and try to force you to bond. Then there was a cookout. At the end of the compulsory festivities, a bunch of kids decided to go hang out on the football field. Tess and I both ended up there. Someone was blasting music and most of the kids were smoking pot, but since that wasn't our scene, Tess and I wandered off together and lay down at the other end of the field, looking at the stars. We didn't even know each other, but we just started talking and something clicked. She told me that she was writing a novel and that I was the only person she had told. And I swear to you, she was barely eighteen years old, but I knew she was serious, that she was the real deal. I remember telling her the novel was going to be extraordinary. And then I told her that I was gay and that she was the only person I had ever told. In my family and culture, it's a crime. She said that life is so unfair and it's hard with family because even when they disappoint us to the core, we still long for their love. Then she said I was a beautiful person and I deserved to live my life fully and authentically. So strange to think about it now, how much trust we had for each other in a matter of moments."

Tess leaned against Jack and he rubbed her arm.

Omar smiled. "Sometimes it happens quickly, I suppose. We just know who the good souls are."

They continued eating and talking for over an hour. Finally, Tess said, "I'm going to make tea and get dessert."

Clay stood up. "I'll help."

When they walked out of the room, Omar quietly said, "That woman hasn't eaten dessert in twenty years, but she always makes sure her guests have everything."

"She's hard on herself," Jack said.

Omar nodded. "If only she could extend to herself what she gives so freely to others."

Soon, Clay returned with a pot of tea and four teacups. Tess placed a platter of bite-size lemon bars, oatmeal raspberry bars, and brownies on the coffee table. "Please, help yourselves," she said.

"Tess, would you like something?" Jack asked.

"I never eat sweets, but all right, just a little," she said, leaning over and selecting an oatmeal raspberry bite, which she promptly nibbled on. "Ooh, that's good. You should try one."

Omar looked at Clay in disbelief.

Jack rubbed Tess's back. "Omar was just about to tell me a funny story about you two at Lincoln Center in New York."

"I can't leave you two alone for a second," Tess replied.

An hour later, Omar and Clay were leaving.

"Tess, you were so sweet to make artichokes. You know they're my favorite," Clay said.

"My pleasure," she replied, hugging him.

"Really great to meet you, Jack," Omar said. He hugged Tess and whispered, "He's wonderful, Butterfly. Be happy."

After they left, Tess put her arms around Jack's neck. "They loved you, like I knew they would."

"They're terrific. I like the way Omar teases you."

"Oh please, don't encourage him."

Jack laughed. "Why does he call you Butterfly?"

"No idea. He's been doing it since we graduated college. I never asked why."

CHAPTER 3

The following Friday night, Jack and Tess made plans for all their closest friends to meet each other. Jack, Joe, Bobby, and Gina arrived at Shelby's Bar first, followed by Tess. Shortly after, Omar and Clay joined them. Tess and Jack made the introductions and ordered the first round of drinks. Soon, they were all talking and laughing like old friends. As the night progressed, the guys shared a few platters of chicken wings and Tess and Gina picked at a Caprese salad.

"That's a pretty necklace," Gina said to Tess.

"Thank you. I wear it every day. It was a gift from Jack," she replied, cozying up against him.

Jack noticed a Middle Eastern man pacing and staring at them from a few feet away, and when they made eye contact, the man approached the table.

He walked up to Omar and asked, "Pardon me, do you speak Arabic?"

"Yes," Omar replied.

He spoke to Omar in Arabic and kept glancing over at Tess. Omar said something in reply and then turned to Tess. "His wife would like to speak to you," he said, gesturing to a woman at a table in the corner. "She doesn't speak English, so he asked me to translate. If you don't want to, it's fine. I'll tell him. You don't have to do this."

Tess looked over at the woman, studying her. "It's okay. I'll talk to her."

Omar relayed the message, and then he and Tess stood up. "Please excuse us," she said.

They walked over and joined the woman at her table.

"I wonder what that's about," Bobby said.

"It seemed to me like maybe Omar didn't want Tess to go. Am I wrong, Clay?" Joe asked.

Clay shrugged. "I'm not sure. He's very protective of her."

Jack didn't take his eyes off Tess. She spoke with the woman for ten minutes and then they embraced. The couple left. Tess walked toward the restrooms and Omar returned to the table.

"Where's Tess?" Jack asked.

"She needed a minute," Omar replied.

"What's going on?" Jack asked.

"I'm sure you all know about Tess's publishing deal and how she owns all the rights to her books, including translation rights. The media wrote all kinds of stories about what a fierce negotiator she is and that her goal was to create a bidding war and raise the price for licensing her work."

Joe nodded. "I read about it at the time."

"Me too," Gina said.

"Tess believes that charity is something you shouldn't shine a spotlight on, so she never corrected the media, but accumulating wealth wasn't her primary motivation. The first thing she did was to give translation rights to nearly every publisher in the Middle East for free. No licensing fees, no royalties, she just gave her work away. She made sure the rights were nonexclusive, so that any publisher who wanted to print and distribute the books would be able to do so, with profit as their motivation. She knew that would flood the market, and hopefully the books would find their way into the hands of those who needed them."

Jack inhaled. "Wow."

"That's truly remarkable," Joe said.

"That's just who Tess is," Omar replied. "But there has been a price to pay. She made some very powerful enemies, as well as scores of brutes who are just plain scary and aren't too keen on women's stories of resilience ending up in the hands and minds of girls and women in their countries."

"Yeah, I bet," Joe said.

"But she expected that type of trouble and doesn't pay any attention to it, even when she should. What she didn't anticipate was what those books would mean to the women who found them. I traveled with her through the Middle East, and you just can't imagine some of the stories that women would tell her about their lives, how they read her books in secret, and what her words mean to them. Even at Heathrow Airport or JFK, women have approached her in public restrooms to share their distressing, personal stories. The woman she just spoke with is from Afghanistan. She told Tess about the daughter of a friend, who was raped by five men. I won't go into all the details, but it was difficult to hear. Before she left, she thanked Tess for her books, told her how much strength and encouragement they provide, and asked her to please keep writing."

"Is Tess okay?" Jack asked.

"She used to hear these kinds of stories hundreds of times a day. She had ways of dealing with it, things she would do to prepare herself to hear the horrors of the world. Of course, each person thinks only of their desire to share their own story, and not the cumulative burden placed on Tess taking in so many people's trauma. I always felt it was terribly unfair of people, but of course Tess doesn't see things that way. About a year ago, she informed everyone she worked with that she wasn't going to do any more public appearances. No explanation. I don't think anything changed, she just decided she was done. But since then, she has a very difficult time when readers approach her, maybe because she hasn't done the mental or spiritual work to prepare for it. I don't know. I just know it hurts her. But still, she won't turn anyone away unless she has a bad feeling about them, and then she won't even shake their hand. It's like she sees something in people's eyes and doesn't know how to look away. She just can't look away. It's some kind of deep-seated call to humanize everyone. It's hard to explain until you see it for yourself." Omar noticed Tess was on her way back to the table. "Please don't say anything. She doesn't like to talk about it."

Everyone nodded.

Tess sat down in the booth next to Jack. He put his hand on her thigh. "You okay?" he whispered.

"Yeah." She turned her attention to the table. "So Bobby, you were going to teach me how to play darts."

***

"You're getting better," Bobby said.

Tess laughed. "I'm terrible, but it's fun."

"I'm not very good either," Gina said, picking up another dart and shooting it at the edge of the board.

"No, you're not," Bobby said with a laugh.

Tess glanced over and saw Jack watching them.

Gina noticed and said, "He's so crazy about you."

"The feeling is mutual," Tess replied.

"We're all so happy for him. He was alone for so long, and then after Gracie, we thought we'd never see him smile again," Gina said.

A look of confusion washed across Tess's face.

"Gina," Bobby mumbled.

"Oh my God, I'm so sorry. I just assumed he told you," Gina said.

Bobby looked at Tess. "Gracie was Jack's daughter. She died about eight months ago. I'm sure he was planning to tell you, but it's really hard for him."

Tess was stunned but managed to say, "That's okay. Please don't say anything to him." They played darts for a little longer until Tess heard the DJ put on "Shallow." "Excuse me," she said, and she walked over to Jack. She took his hand. "It's a slow one. Dance with me?"

He got up and followed her to the dance floor. They pressed their bodies together, melting into each other. When the song was over, Tess whispered, "Let's stay at your place tonight."

***

When they got to Jack's apartment, he went to grab a couple glasses of water. Tess sat down on the couch and noticed a pile of her books on the coffee table.

Jack sat down next to her. "I ordered your books."

"Yeah, I can see that."

"I've been reading them on my lunch break. I'm on the second one. Tess, you're so talented. They're incredible."

She smiled.

"I was surprised you wanted to stay here tonight," he said. "We've been at your place all week."

"I thought you might be more comfortable," she said, putting her hand on his thigh. "I need to talk to you about something." She glanced down.

He took her hands in his. "What is it?"

"Gina told me about Gracie. She didn't mean to. She didn't realize I didn't know."

Jack looked down and took a deep breath. "I'm sorry," he said. "I… I wasn't trying to keep it from you. It's just that I never had to tell anyone before."

"You don't have to be sorry. Do you want to tell me now?"

He took a moment to gather himself and then he began talking. "Until I took a desk job about a year ago, I didn't think I could be in a relationship. My job was too intense, too dangerous, too unpredictable. But sometimes I'd meet someone in a bar for a night. That's how I met her mother. It was just one night, five years ago. She never told me she was pregnant. I didn't know I was a father until about eight months ago when she contacted me. She told me about Gracie and that she was sick." He stopped as his eyes flooded with tears. Tess rubbed his back. He wiped the tears away and continued. "She had leukemia and needed a bone marrow transplant. Her mother wanted me to get tested." He paused. "But she was too sick. It was too late. There was nothing they could do. I spent eleven days in the hospital with her and then she died. I only knew her for eleven days and she didn't even know who I was." He began sobbing.

"You said you once took two weeks off from work. That was why," Tess said.

"Yes," he mumbled through tears. "I slept at the hospital for eleven days, by her side."

"I'm so sorry, Jack. What was Gracie like?"

"She was an angel. She loved the color purple and she had the sweetest laugh."

"Do you have a picture of her?"

Jack got up and went into his bedroom. He returned with two photographs.

"She's beautiful," Tess said.

"She didn't look like this when I knew her. She was so frail and had lost her hair, but she was still beautiful. Her mother gave me these so I could see what she had been like."

"Do you keep in touch with her mother?"

Jack shook his head. "At first, I was so angry with her. But then I realized, I realized…"

She rubbed his back. "What?"

"It was my fault, it was all my fault," he said, doubling over and bursting into tears.

"It's wasn't your fault, Jack. Why do you think that?"

"She never told me about Gracie because she didn't want me in their lives. I never led anyone on or treated anyone badly, but I must have done something wrong because she never even told me she was pregnant. Maybe it was because of my stupid job; I told her how dangerous it was. But it was my fault, my fault she didn't want me to know about her or be in her life. It was my fault she didn't tell me in time so that I could save her," he said, his body rocking back and forth as he sobbed.

"Oh baby, it wasn't your fault. It wasn't your fault. You didn't do anything wrong." He couldn't stop crying. Tess threw her arms around him. "I've got you. It's okay. I've got you."

A few minutes later, Jack was finally able to take a deep breath and stop sobbing. He wiped his eyes and looked up at Tess. "I never thought I could have this kind of happiness until I met you, especially after Gracie. I love you so much and I don't ever want to lose you. I'll do anything for you."

"Jack, I never truly felt safe or happy until I met you. You're everything to me. I'm right here, and I'm not going anywhere."

CHAPTER 4

After spending every night together, Jack and Tess met their friends at Shelby's Bar the next Friday night, taking what had already become their usual table by the dance floor. They spent the evening talking and laughing like they had known each other for years. Tess noticed that Omar kept checking his phone and seemed disconnected from the group. She picked up a pretzel and tossed it at him.

"All work and no play makes Omar a big bore."

"He's worse than I am when I'm on call," Clay said.

Omar shot them each a look.

"I was promised a night of fun and dancing. I don't care about anything else," Tess said, picking up another pretzel and flinging it at him.

Omar intercepted it midair. "If you do that again, you're going to wear that basket," he teased.

"See, isn't this more fun than staring at your phone?" Tess asked, smiling mischievously.

"Butterfly, I'm doing this for you. The final offer is going to come in any minute, and I promised I'd get a response from you right away," Omar said. "Ah, and here it is!" He put his phone down and looked at Tess. "They're up to five point five plus a cut of merchandising, and they're still offering a producer credit, although I know you're not interested. It's an A-level deal. This is as good as it gets. I spoke with Larry directly. He wants this to happen; he's already clearing space on his mantel for the awards."

"Is he?" Tess asked.

"Everyone is hoping you'll give the green light before the weekend."

"It's already the weekend," Tess protested.

"They're on LA time."

Tess picked up a pretzel and started picking off the grains of salt, one by one.

"Butterfly, you know I wouldn't press you, but this has dragged on for ages and we can finally close it. No one will be comfortable until you give the word. They know how you are."

She shot him a look.

"What is it?" Omar asked.

"I don't like this bleeding into my time with Jack and our friends."

"Then why didn't you accept the offer they made two days ago, or the one this morning? We both know this will end with a phone call between you and Larry anyway. You could have called him earlier."

"That offer wasn't a good starting point for the conversation. Besides, maybe I don't want to do it at all."

Omar sighed. "If that's really the case, I'll tell them to fuck off."

"You would not," Tess said, gleefully.

"If that's what you want, yes I would. Just say the word."

Tess picked up another pretzel, rolling it around in her fingers.

"Please call Larry. He's at the studio with his legal team on standby. You do know he's the head of a major studio, right Butterfly? He doesn't wait around for most people."

Tess nuzzled closer to Jack.

Omar raised his eyebrows.

"You're impossible. Okay, I'll call him." She looked up at Jack. "I'm sorry, baby. I'll be right back."

He kissed her and she excused herself from the table.

Omar turned to Clay. "She's not going to accept the deal. I could see it in her eyes when I said the number. It's a world-class offer." He looked at Jack. "I'm sorry. It's my fault. She never conducts business when she's with friends. Bloody hell, we can't even get her to answer her cell phone, which is maddening. I'm sure she'll give me grief later."

"It's fine," Jack said. "Tess can do whatever she needs to do. What's it all about, anyway?"

"It's for the film rights to one of her books. We've worked with this studio before. We have a good relationship with them, and it will be worth the licensing price many times over once you consider the ripple effect."

"That's so exciting," Gina said. "I've seen all the movies they've adapted from her books. *Blue Moon* is my favorite movie of all time. Does Tess have a favorite?"

Omar laughed. "She's never seen any of them."

"Are you serious?" Joe asked.

"Yeah. If you ask her, she'll tell you that she doesn't have to see the film because she's read the book."

Jack laughed.

"Tess has a very personal relationship with her books. She never discusses the characters and what they mean to her. I think she prefers to let them live in her imagination as she created them," Omar said.

"Tell me: Tess is so sweet. Do people try to take advantage of her?" Jack asked.

"I pity anyone who does," Omar replied with a chuckle and a shake of his head. "Her debut novel became an international bestseller when she was barely twenty-two. Within a year, she was signing her landmark publishing deal, for which she was the sole architect. Afterward, she put together a small team of advisors and asked me to be there for support. She asked a trademark lawyer to explain some specifics to her, but instead of explaining, he tried to tell her what to do. She said, 'I'm not asking for your advice; I'm asking for an education.' He said that he didn't want to waste time. She said, 'I have time and I'm paying for your time. What's the issue? Do you think you're not capable of teaching me, or that I'm not capable of learning?' Before he could respond, she calmly said, 'Thank you, but your services are no longer needed.' He was floored. She set the tone then and there. And I'll tell you, now that woman knows more about intellectual property law than most attorneys."

Jack laughed.

Omar continued, "Many people tried to convince her to focus on her art and leave the business to others, but she was having none of it. She didn't want to be at the mercy of the men who run this industry. Anyone who ever suggested that she couldn't be both a great artist and a fierce businesswoman was sorely mistaken. If you ever want to see something truly impressive, watch her run a meeting. She never loses her kindness, but she's in complete control. Just the other day, we were having our weekly video conference with her team. Someone made a suggestion that she didn't agree with. After hearing them out, she calmly but firmly said no. A few minutes later, he attempted to repackage his advice. She stopped him and said, 'I already said no. No is a complete sentence.' When the meeting was over, she dissolved any lingering tension by asking about his wife, who recently got a promotion. No one takes advantage of Tess, nor does she ever lose herself."

Jack smiled.

Omar continued, "I'll bet you that right now, she's either breaking Larry's heart by turning down the deal or she's getting the price up. Either way, I guarantee that she asks about his kids. Of course, she only cares about the price because she's planning to give it all away, otherwise it wouldn't matter to her. Tess's only blind spot is self-care. When she first started touring, she had a laundry list of requirements. There had to be access for people with disabilities anywhere she spoke, she insisted on being interviewed by people of color, and on and on. But she wouldn't put simple things like water in her rider. One convention manager actually had to ask, 'Does Ms. Lee want something to drink in the green room?' I asked Tess and she was like, 'Oh yeah, water would be fine.' I asked her what kind and she said it didn't matter. That's when I decided to travel with her whenever possible, so I could look out for her."

"Have you ever regretted changing your life that way?" Jack asked.

"Not for a second. Tess leads an extraordinary life and I've been lucky to be a part of it. My only regret is that I've enjoyed it more than she has."

The conversation moved on, and fifteen minutes later, Tess returned to the table. She slid back into the booth beside Jack. He put his arm around her. "I missed you," she whispered.

"I missed you, too," he replied.

Everyone stared at her expectantly. Omar's eyes were like saucers. "Well?" he asked.

"Seven point two plus a cut of merchandising," she said, matter-of-factly.

Omar grinned from ear to ear. He raised his glass. Tess picked up her glass and they clinked. "Holy hell, you are brilliant, Butterfly. How did you possibly manage that?"

Tess's expression turned serious. "Perhaps I told him he was buying a piece of my soul, and I asked him what he might consider a fair price for a piece of his soul."

Omar furrowed his brow, picked up a pretzel, and lobbed it at her. "How did you really do it?"

Tess smirked. "They're going to donate twenty percent of it to a mutually agreed upon charity, which is a great tax break for them and good PR, at my suggestion. We'll match the donation."

Omar laughed. "Well done."

"Oh, and he said hi to you," Tess continued. "His older daughter decided to major in psychology. I told him you'd be a resource."

Omar glanced at Jack and they both smiled.

"Am I off the clock now? Have I sufficiently earned my keep?" Tess asked.

"Does this mean it's a bad time to ask if you've reconsidered the invitation to judge that beauty pageant?" Omar joked.

Tess got ready to throw the whole basket of pretzels.

He laughed. "Yes, Butterfly. You're free."

"Good, because I was promised a night of dancing, and so far, there has been no dancing."

Everyone congratulated Tess on the deal and the conversation moved on. Jack leaned over and whispered, "Come with me." He took Tess's hand and led her to the hallway near the restrooms, the quietest spot in the bar.

"What you said to Omar was true; I could hear it in your voice. That's how you feel when you sell your work, like you're selling a piece of your soul."

Her eyes became watery. "Yes," she said softly.

He pulled her close.

"Jack?"

"Yeah, baby."

"Do you think it's possible for two people to know each other completely?"

"Yes. I do," he replied, brushing the side of her face.

***

When the DJ showed up, Tess, Gina, and Clay got up to dance. The others watched as the trio let loose to a string of pub favorites. Eventually they tired and rejoined the group. Tess cozied up to Jack.

"Jack, you're as bad as Bobby. He won't dance with me either. Thank God for Clay," Gina said.

"I stick to the slow songs," Jack replied.

When the unmistakable opening piano notes of "All of Me" came on, Tess looked up at Jack. "It's our song, baby."

"That's my cue," he said to the group.

He led her onto the dance floor. She put one hand on his shoulder, and he slipped one around her waist to the small of her back. They started to sway, staring at each other as if they were the only people in the world. As the song progressed, she moved her hand down his arm to pull him closer, and he ran his fingers through her hair. They were pressed tightly together, in slow movement. Everyone at their table watched, smiles across their faces.

"Whoa," Bobby mumbled.

"They are really in love. I've never seen anything like it," Joe said.

Clay put his arm around Omar and said, "Look at them."

"If I didn't see it with my own eyes, I'd never believe it. My sweet Butterfly is truly happy."

When the song was over, Jack whispered, "Let's go to your place."

***

At the end of the evening, they all bundled up and stumbled out of the bar.

A homeless man standing on the sidewalk asked, "Can you please spare anything?"

The group stood around awkwardly, but Tess walked right up to him. "Hi. I'm Tess, this is Jack, and these are our friends."

Jack stepped directly behind Tess in a protective stance.

"What's your name?" Tess gently asked the man.

"Henry," he replied.

She smiled, pulled a twenty dollar bill out of her pocket, and handed it to him. When he took the money, she held his hand. Surprised, he looked at her and said, "You're very kind. Thank you."

"Getting kind of cold out," she said, still holding his hand.

"Sure is."

She took off her cashmere scarf and held it out. "Here, please take this and try to stay warm."

"Wow," Joe muttered.

"Oh, I couldn't," Henry said.

"Please, I insist."

"Thank you," he said, taking the scarf. "Someone must have taught you to do unto others."

"No, someone taught me there are no others. Goodnight, Henry."

She turned to her friends, their mouths agape.

Henry looked at Jack, who hadn't moved, and quietly asked, "Is she some kind of angel?"

"Yeah, something like that," he muttered.

Tess walked over to Omar and hugged him. "Our usual breakfast on Thursday?"

"Yes, Butterfly."

"Goodnight, guys," she said to her friends.

They all said goodnight. Jack took Tess's hand and walked her to his car. He opened her door and she got in. When he closed the door, he looked back at Henry, who was wrapping the scarf around his neck and smiling.

***

Tess removed her coat and shoes as Jack locked the door. He kicked off his shoes and threw his jacket on the countertop. He came up behind Tess, put his hands around her waist, and she turned to face him. Without a word, they started to kiss passionately. He picked her up, carried her to the bedroom, and put her down on the edge of the bed. They both pulled their shirts off. Jack grabbed a pillow and placed it behind Tess. He lay her down, pulled off the rest of her clothes, and took off his own. He started at her feet, gently kissing her, and worked his way up her body. Soon, they were making love. After, they lay beside each other, kissing. Jack pulled a blanket over them.

"I'm sorry," he said. "I couldn't wait another minute."

"I'm so happy. I've never felt anything like this before."

"Me either."

"Why don't you move in with me? I want to wake up each morning with you and fall asleep in your arms each night."

"Marry me, Tess."

"Are you serious?"

"I've never been more serious in my life. I love you with my whole heart. Marry me."

"Yes," she whispered. "I'll marry you."

CHAPTER 5

Jack pulled into a parking space. "Ready?"

"Do you think Omar will be happy for us?" Tess asked, fidgeting. She was obviously nervous.

"I hope so."

"But what if he isn't?"

"How he feels means a lot to you."

"Yes. I would be heartbroken if…"

He squeezed her hand. "I promise I'll do everything I can to show him how much I love you."

She took a deep breath. "Okay, let's go."

***

The waitress served their drinks and asked, "Are you ready to order?"

"I think we need a few more minutes," Jack said.

Omar held up his mimosa. "Brunch is my favorite meal."

"That's because it's just breakfast with cocktails," Tess said.

"Exactly," he replied.

"Me too," Gina added. "This place is really cute. We've never been here before," she said, touching Bobby's hand.

"I've been coming here for years. Glad you like it," Joe said.

"Clay sends his regrets. Life of a surgeon, you know. So Tess, to what do we owe? Twice in one weekend. When you invited us to brunch, you said you had news. Something we can toast to?" Omar asked.

"As a matter of fact, yes," she replied. She turned to Jack. "Go ahead."

He put his arm around Tess. "We're getting married."

"Oh my God, that's so exciting!" Gina exclaimed.

"Wow, congratulations," Joe said.

"Yeah, wow. Congratulations, you two," Bobby said, raising his glass. "That's awesome."

"Omar?" Tess asked.

"Oh, Butterfly, I'm so happy for you," he said, jumping up and rushing over to hug her. "You're perfect for each other," he whispered. When he finally let go of Tess, Jack stood up and shook his hand.

"Congratulations. You're a lucky man," Omar said.

"Thank you. I know it."

When they all sat down, Omar raised his glass. "Well this is certainly worthy of a toast. To Tess and Jack! I wish you every happiness."

"Cheers!"

"So? When's the big day?" Joe asked.

"Saturday," Tess replied.

Omar choked on his drink. "Saturday, as in six days from now?"

"Yes, so I'll need your help," Tess replied.

"Butterfly, I know you're a writer, but must everything always be so dramatic? Why so fast?" Omar asked.

She rolled her eyes. "Because we've already waited a lifetime. It's going to be small, at our place, a private ceremony at five o'clock followed by a cocktail party at eight. We're only having about forty or fifty people. I already called everyone yesterday, and Crystal is booking flights and hotels, and making arrangements for those flying private. But I could really use your help. Since Clay is at the hospital today, we were hoping you could come over after brunch. Pretty please?"

Omar smiled. "Of course. Whatever you need."

"Oh, and don't flip out, but I'm legally changing my name," Tess said.

"Your publisher will love that," Omar joked.

Tess crinkled her nose. "Relax, I'll still use Tess Lee for work. But Omar, I'll finally have a real name."

He smiled.

"What do you mean?" Bobby asked.

"She was born Esther Leopold. Her family called her Essie," Omar said.

Tess shuddered. "I hated it. When I left home, I changed it to Tess Lee. But now I'll be Tess Miller, except on my books."

"You better lead with that when you tell your publisher," Omar said.

Tess giggled.

***

After the waitress took their orders, a tall, thin woman with straggly brown hair approached their table. "Excuse me, are you Tess Lee?" she asked.

Everyone turned to look.

Jack put his arm across the back of Tess's chair.

"Yes," Tess replied.

"I don't want to bother you, but…" she said nervously.

"You're not bothering me," Tess assured her.

The woman's eyes became teary. "I've read all your novels. The last one, *Shadows*," she said, pausing before continuing, "that scene with the cereal." Her voice became quieter and more sincere. "There was a time I felt that way. Things are better now, but it's still hard sometimes. I keep that book on my nightstand. Some mornings, I reread that scene and the last line of the book. It helps me. I just wanted to say thank you."

Tess looked at her sympathetically and took the woman's hand. "You're very kind. I'm glad it helps."

When the woman walked away, Jack whispered in Tess's ear, "Are you okay?"

She just nodded.

"I haven't had a chance to read your last book yet. What scene was she talking about?" Joe asked.

"I used to hear people talk about 'good' or 'bad' times to receive news, and I always thought that was strange. Is there really a *good* time for someone to tell you that they're ill, they've cheated on you, they're an addict, someone is hurting them, or they want to die? Why is one time better than another? And so many people don't really hear the difficult things their loved ones tell them. I've always included scenes in my novels where the character is having an interior monologue about something they want to confess but never do, or scenes where someone musters the courage to share their darkest secret, but the other person doesn't truly hear them. Sometimes, I set these scenes in absurd places, like a woman buying cotton candy at a carnival and revealing that her boyfriend beats her. Other times, I set the scenes amid the everyday minutia of life. As a writer, I love the everyday, small stuff."

"Is that why you're so insane about refusing to get your groceries delivered or hiring a chef or any of the other things I've suggested to free up your time for more important matters?" Omar asked, taking a swill of his cocktail.

"How can I write about normal, daily life if I don't experience it?" Tess replied.

"Bloody hell, you've been to the grocery store before. How much do you think it's changed?" he asked with a laugh.

She shot him a look.

"Sorry, Butterfly. Please go on."

"The woman who came over was talking about a passage where the protagonist reveals something very dark, but her boyfriend is too preoccupied with his breakfast. When he finally does listen, he fails to hear the gravity of her words. I know it by heart, if you want to hear it. I remember it in detail because the moment I wrote it, I decided not to do book signings anymore."

"Please, we'd love to hear it," Joe said. Everyone else echoed their agreement.

"I'll give you a little background. The protagonist is terribly lonely. She's dating this guy, but he's kind of a loser. Their whole relationship is sad. Their apartment is sad, the sex they have is sad, even their hair is a bit dirty. There's just a veneer of sadness over everything. He doesn't understand who she is. She's desperate to make it work, just to have a human connection, so she summons all her courage to tell him something important. He's sitting at the Formica kitchen table, eating a bowl of Fruit Loops, and she comes in and sits across from him. The scene goes like this:

> "Can you stop eating for a minute? I need to talk
> to you," she says.

"It'll get soggy," he responds, not even looking up from his bowl.

"I'll wait," she says. She watched him slurp each bite, listened to every munching sound, which reverberated like a jackhammer. Those minutes felt longer than all the minutes that had come before.

He finished eating, plunked his spoon down into the remnant pink milk, and looked at her. "Well? What is it?"

"Every morning when I wake up, the first thing I think to myself is: today I can die. Without that thought, without knowing I can end it, I couldn't bear to get up. I lie in bed and think of all the ways I can die. First, I think that I want to crawl into a hole. No thought brings me more comfort than picturing myself buried in the ground, but I can't figure out how to do it by myself. I would fail. I can't fail again. So then, I wish my body was like a lobster's. I imagine someone splitting me down the middle, cracking my back, pulling off my limbs, and scooping out my insides. The thought brings relief, but it's unrealistic, so I start to think about things that are possible. I could get a gun, slit my wrists, or hang myself from that flickering light in the closet. But I'm a coward, this I know. Maybe I should jump off a bridge, that bridge just outside of town, the rusty one. I think it's high enough, but I'm not sure. I wonder if I'll feel my body crashing against the water? Will my bones break? And then I wonder, when I leap, should I close my eyes or keep them open? I can't decide. Until I know that, I'm stuck, so I move on with the day. Every morning, I wage this war before you even get out of bed. It always begins the same way. I think to myself: today I can die." She inhaled, eyes wide, waiting for a response.

He sat for a moment, looking at her, and then said, "It would be easier to just think: Today I can live."

He got up and brought his bowl to the sink. She sat dumbfounded. *Today I can live.* That thought had never occurred to her.

Jack leaned over and kissed Tess on the cheek.

"It's a wonderful novel," Gina said. "I've read it twice. They break up shortly after that scene, but the last line of the book is everything."

"What's the last line?" Joe asked.

Tess gestured at Gina that she should go ahead. "On this morning, she rose to the smell of coffee, the taste of possibility, and a singular thought: *today I can live*."

"Wow," Bobby muttered.

"Butterfly, I never pushed because I knew how exhausted you were at the time, your schedule was maddening, and you never listened to me when I suggested slowing down. But I've always wanted to know: why did you stop making public appearances?" Omar asked.

"You know better than anyone what my life was like: all planes, drivers, and hotels. For so long, I avoided being still, planting roots."

"It seemed like you were on a mission," Omar said.

Tess nodded her head. "That's how it went in my mind, too. I wanted to give everything I could."

"What happened?" Omar asked.

"The writing itself takes a toll. I feel what each character feels. Even when I move on from the book, a residue remains. Then add everything else on top of that. By the end, I thought I might shatter into a million pieces if I heard one more of their stories. You know what it was like. Hundreds of readers a day, for months on end, year after year. When I wrote the cereal scene, I knew I would hear things like what that woman said. Without you all here, it would have been more intense. I just couldn't do it anymore, even with all the tricks I had learned to cope. Besides, so much of it never felt real to me. Being trotted out like a prize horse didn't suit me."

"What do you mean?" Joe asked.

"You should have heard the way they would introduce me at all the events, all hyperbole and nonsense. I wasn't comfortable with it. The more so-called success I attained, the worse it became."

"I know, Butterfly, but there were good things too. Some of the places we saw and the people we met. We had fun," Omar said.

"It was different when you were there," Tess said.

Omar smiled and looked around the table. "You guys should have seen the places she held talks. The crowds stood in line for hours, waiting to see her." He turned his gaze toward Tess. "The cathedral in Barcelona was amazing, ooh, and that garden in Budapest! Or when they put you in that packed arena in Singapore, with those drones flying overhead. You must admit, there were some spectacular experiences. What was your favorite? There must have been something that felt real."

Tess laughed. "I have a favorite. You weren't there and it wasn't glamorous. It was about seven years ago. I was doing a US book tour and we stopped in Kansas for two days. I was scheduled to do a book signing at a local store the first night and a public talk at the university the next day. The whole trip was a nightmare. I decided not to take my jet because I didn't want the solitude, but flying commercial turned out to be a huge mistake. There was a weather event and the plane ride was awful. People were violently sick. I'm a highly experienced traveler and even I wasn't doing well by the time we arrived. Then, my driver informed me that almost everything was shut down because of the weather. People were advised to stay at home, but the bookstore owner decided to remain open. She had ordered crateloads of books, expecting a line out the door. I felt badly for her, so I agreed to brave the weather and do the signing. Only seven people showed up."

"Seriously?" Bobby asked.

"Yeah, literally seven people. The owner was mortified. I never cared about how many people came to anything, so it didn't bother me. I thought it was kind of great. Since there were so few people, I had plenty of time to talk with each one. There was a man named Brad, about thirty years old, and he had a copy of *Candy Floss* with him that he asked me to sign. Men don't usually approach me about that book, so I was curious, but I just signed it. He told me that he was a single father of a little girl, Ava. Her mother wasn't in the picture. Ava was obviously everything to him. He glowed when he spoke about her. He told me that she thought she was ugly and she would cry about it, which broke his heart. He didn't know what to do. He said that he read my book, and for the first time, he understood how she felt and why she felt that way. He thanked me profusely and said the book made him a better father."

"That's so sweet," Jack said.

Tess nodded. "Before my talk at the university the next day, I was up at the podium making sure everything was all set. Brad walked into the auditorium holding a little girl, who was maybe four or five. I walked toward them. Ava was curled up against him, the most beautiful, most perfect child I'd ever seen. She has Down syndrome."

Everyone at the table let out an audible sigh.

"Brad said that my book helped them so much and he wanted me to meet her. He said she was shy, but when he put her down, I knelt on the floor and she leapt into my arms and hugged me tightly. *That* felt real. We still keep in touch. I send them signed books. Ava's doing great."

Jack took Tess's hand under the table.

"Don't you ever miss it? The travel or meeting readers?" Bobby asked.

"I did it for them, not for me. And it was too much."

"But Butterfly, it doesn't have to be that way. Instead of spending months traveling, you could do a few signings a year if you wanted. You could choose. Heaven knows your publisher would be thrilled if you'd just do a couple of events."

"Why do you care anyway?" she asked.

"Because I don't want you to be less than you are."

Tess looked down.

Omar continued. "You could go to New York, your favorite place. You used to spend so much time there, you must miss it," Omar said.

She shrugged. "Honestly, I don't want to sacrifice any time with Jack. Not even for a day. That's what means the most to me. Please respect that."

"I could go with you," Jack said. "If there was something you wanted to do, I can take time off."

"This guy needs a vacation," Bobby said. "He's been a workaholic for too long."

"He's right," Joe concurred.

Tess smiled.

"Promise me you'll think about it, Butterfly. It could be on your terms," Omar said.

Just then, brunch was served and everyone focused on their food. Tess picked up her fork, and Jack leaned over and whispered, "I meant what I said. It's fine if you're done with public events, but if you change your mind, I'll be there."

She smiled and said, "I know, and I love you."

* * *

Tess brought a pot of tea into the living room where Jack and Omar were sitting.

"Thank you so much for coming over to help," Tess said to Omar. "You're the only one who knows all the guests, and you can imagine the madness with this eclectic crew. I'm going to run up to the office to print out the guest list and details."

Tess flew out of the room. As soon as she was gone, Omar said, "I'm glad we have a moment alone. I was hoping to talk to you privately."

"Okay," Jack said.

"You haven't known Tess very long, and now you're getting married, and…"

Jack interrupted him. "She was so nervous about telling you."

"Tess doesn't get nervous," Omar said.

"She did about this. Your approval means the world to her. I love her. I love her with my whole heart, and I promise I always will."

Omar shook his head. "You misunderstand. I'm truly happy for you both. I knew from the first moment I saw you two that you belong together. Anyone can see how much you love each other. I understand that it can happen quickly; I knew right away with Clay. It took me a while to convince him, but I knew."

Jack laughed.

"All I have ever wanted was for Tess to find the love that she deserves so she can finally enjoy this incredible life she has created for herself. But there's something you need to know about her."

"I'm listening."

"I don't want this to come out wrong. Tess is the strongest, most brilliant person I have ever known. But there is something fragile in her."

"I know," Jack said softly. "I see it in her eyes."

"She's hugely kind to others, but not to herself. Tess needs someone to take care of her and look out for her so that she can soar as she's meant to. She needs to feel love, every day. I'm asking you to please do that for her."

"I promise I will."

Tess returned, a stack of papers in hand. She plopped down on the couch next to Jack. "So, what have I missed?"

"We were just talking about how much we love you," Jack said.

"Ah, well I hope you still feel that way when you see your list of tasks."

CHAPTER 6

Tess was in the kitchen dusting off platters when Jack came home, Joe in tow. "I missed you," she said.

"Missed you too," he said, giving her a kiss. "Sorry we're late. I stopped to pick this up for tomorrow," Jack said, handing her a box with a bridal bouquet of white hydrangeas.

She smiled. "It's so beautiful. Thank you."

He took the box back and put it in the refrigerator.

"I got you a wedding present, too," she said.

"You didn't have to do that," he replied, turning to face her.

"I wanted to." She took his hands and said, "I made a small donation to pediatric cancer research in Gracie's name. It's symbolic, really."

Jack choked back his tears and took a breath. "That's the nicest thing you could have ever given me. Thank you. I love you so much." He wiped his eyes and kissed the top of her head.

"Well, we should get some plates out. Dinner will be here soon," she said, brushing his forehead with her hand.

He sniffled and turned to Joe. "Can I get you a beer?"

"Sure," Joe said. "Tess, are you sure you guys wouldn't rather be alone tonight?"

"Absolutely. We're just getting pizza and salad delivered. Omar will be here any minute. Please stay."

"All right," Joe said. "Thank you."

The doorbell rang. Jack hit the buzzer and opened the door for Omar, who was holding a cake box.

"Hello, hello! The wedding cake is here," he said, kissing Tess on the cheek and whizzing past her to the refrigerator.

"You know I don't eat cake," Tess said.

"Think of your guests, Butterfly. We want cake," Omar responded, opening the refrigerator. "Oh dear, you haven't even made room," he said, placing the box on the counter while he shuffled food around.

"Sorry, I was busy today," Tess replied.

"Oh yes, I heard all about your treachery. First, you threaten to fire the lawyers, and now you're giving poor Barry an ulcer. I'm telling you, that man is drinking Mylanta by the bottle."

Tess tried to make a noise and shake her head to get him to stop talking, but with his back turned, he didn't notice and continued. "Did you really have to threaten to fire him again? I mean, he is an accountant, Butterfly. Even with your usual over-the-top generosity, don't you think an anonymous eleven million dollar donation warranted him oh, I don't know, pausing to make sure you hadn't gone completely mad?"

"Oh, Omar," she whispered.

"Wow," Joe mumbled.

"What? Eleven million dollars?" Jack muttered. "A *small* donation?"

Tess turned to face him. His eyes flooded. In a hushed tone she said, "It's small in comparison to what you lost. Each day you had together is worth far more than a million dollars. Maybe it will help other parents and children have more days together. Are you upset?"

"Upset?" he asked softly. He wrapped his arms around her and touched his forehead to hers. "No, sweetheart. I'm… I'm at a loss for words."

"My whole life is words. I'm grateful we don't need them," she replied.

He smiled through his tears and gently kissed her. Then she rested her head on his chest and cuddled into him. No sounds, no words.

***

"Well, this bride-to-be needs her beauty sleep. I'm going to bed. Thank you both for coming over. You're all set on where everything goes tomorrow?"

"Yes," Omar said. "We'll be on top of everything. Joe and I will be here at five to be your witnesses, and then you two can spend some time together while we deal with the caterers and bartender. Oh, and I'll make sure the security guard has the guest list at the door. Don't worry Butterfly, it's all set. Your every wish is my command. By the time you and Jack emerge at eight o'clock, everything will be perfect and you can enjoy your guests."

"Thank you. I love you," she said, hugging him. She pecked Joe on the cheek and headed to her bedroom.

"I'll be there in a few minutes, sweetheart," Jack said.

"Goodnight, guys. See you tomorrow," Joe said as he left.

"Omar, can I please talk to you for a minute?" Jack asked.

"Of course. What is it?"

"Earlier, you said that Tess threatened to fire her lawyers. Why?"

Omar fidgeted and looked away.

"Please, tell me," Jack said.

"They drew up a prenuptial agreement they wanted you to sign. She went nuts. She didn't want you to know about it."

"Do you have it? I'll sign it."

"It's in my car. But Jack, she doesn't want you to sign it. It offends her. All she hears when it's mentioned is that you might not be together forever. She can't bear that. She would never leave you."

"And I'm never going to leave her. I promised her forever and I meant it."

"She doesn't care about money, and honestly, I just want her to be happy. You make her happy, Jack. No one who knows you or has seen the two of you together thinks it matters."

"It matters to me. You asked me to take care of her. I gave you my word that I would, and that's what I'm trying to do. Please, just get it. She doesn't need to know about it."

"I don't keep things from Tess, especially not when they concern her," Omar said.

"I know, and normally I wouldn't ask. Please, help me do the right thing."

Omar nodded and went to retrieve the document. When he returned, he handed it to Jack, who was waiting with a pen. He flipped to each page with a signature flag and signed it.

"Don't you think you should have a lawyer review that, or at least read it yourself?" Omar asked.

"I told you, I'm never going to leave her."

"Then why insist on signing it?" Omar asked.

"Because she deserves for the men in her life to protect her. I hope she stays with me forever, but it needs to be her choice. Here," he said, handing back the document. "Please sign the witness line and see it gets to where it needs to go. Keep this between us."

Omar nodded. "It's not legally binding without her signature."

"Now she'll always be able to sign it, if she chooses."

"Do you know what she told me after your first weekend together? She said, 'He sees me, and I see him. I trust him completely, like I always did with you.' Then when you gave her that necklace, she FaceTimed me so I could see it. She was prattling on like a schoolgirl about how much she loves you, and then she said, 'He makes me feel like I'm enough, exactly as I am.' Tess has never felt that way before."

Jack smiled.

"I know you think you're lucky to be with her, but I want you to know that from the day I first met you, I knew she was also lucky to be with you. You're a good man. I'm thrilled you found each other."

Jack extended his hand. "Thank you. That means a lot to me."

CHAPTER 7

Their wedding day had finally arrived. Jack wore his finest suit and waited with Joe and the justice of the peace.

Tess came out wearing a simple, strapless white gown with a sweetheart neckline and her gold heart locket, her hair cascading in loose, spiral curls. Jack covered his heart with his hands. "You are breathtaking. I can't wait to marry you."

She handed her bouquet to Omar and they began the ceremony. Face to face and hand in hand, they recited the vows they had each written.

Jack said, "I've seen a lot of the bad in this world, and you are everything that's good. Since joining the military nearly twenty-five years ago, I've given one hundred percent of my loyalty and dedication to my job. Now I want to give that same level of commitment to you. I promise to love, honor, and protect you for all the days of my life. Tess, you are my world. I love you with my whole heart, forever."

Tess said, "People often say that I have everything, but I've never had the one thing I truly longed for until I met you: happiness. Jack, you are the best thing that has ever happened to me. You are my joy, my strength, and my heart. You're my missing piece and I'm yours. I love you with every fiber of my soul and I always will."

They both wiped away tears.

Jack turned to the justice of the peace and said, "You better hurry up because I need to kiss her."

They exchanged rings and were pronounced "husband and wife." They kissed as if no one was there. They thanked the justice of the peace. Jack shook Joe and Omar's hands and Tess hugged them both.

"You and Jack are perfect together. I wish you every happiness, Butterfly," Omar whispered. He then insisted on taking a few photographs of the newlyweds, despite the bride's complaints.

With Omar and Joe in charge of handling the incoming staff, Jack and Tess excused themselves to spend their first hours as a married couple alone. When they got to their bedroom door, Jack picked Tess up and carried her across the threshold. He put her down and said, "I'm the luckiest person alive."

She said, "That's exactly how I feel."

After making love, they sat in bed, snuggling and talking about the party.

"So, what do I need to know about your guests?" Tess asked.

"It's just the folks from my group at work. They're all good people. There is this one guy, Chris, who's kind of a jerk. He wanted my job and resents me. Everyone else is cool. What about your friends?"

"Oh, it's sort of a random group. My publisher, Claire, my assistant, Crystal, and then a smattering of friends from all over. A hair stylist, an actress, a singer. I mainly want you to meet my friend Abdul and his wife. Abdul is very special to me."

"Tell me about him," Jack said.

"I would rather let you meet him for yourself. But I will tell you that he is one of the people I respect most in this world. He's also one of the only people who I feel really understands me. He has a slow, considered way of speaking. I hang on every wise word. I can't wait for you to meet."

"Then I can't wait to meet him."

Tess looked at the clock. "Honey, we'd better get dressed before our guests arrive."

"Just one more minute. I want to kiss my wife."

When they were finally able to tear themselves out of bed, Tess changed into a sleek black jumpsuit with a plunging neckline, and as always, her heart locket. Jack wore black slacks and a lightweight black sweater. They left their room just before eight, and as promised, Omar and Joe had taken care of everything. They were ready to greet their guests.

CHAPTER 8

"Is that the actress from…" Bobby began to ask.

Jack nodded.

"Didn't she win an Oscar last year?" Bobby asked.

"Wow, Tess has quite an impressive and diverse group of friends," Joe said. "Who's that woman she's speaking to?"

"A good friend from New York. They met waiting in line for a concert," Jack replied.

Joe laughed. "She really is one of a kind."

Just then, Chris walked over and shook Jack's hand. "Congratulations. You've certainly done well for yourself."

Bobby rolled his eyes. Before Jack could respond, Tess flitted over. She kept one hand in her pocket and intertwined her other arm with Jack's.

"Sweetheart, this is Chris. We work together."

"A pleasure to meet you," Chris said.

"Likewise," Tess replied.

"I was just congratulating Jack. He certainly married up," Chris said.

"Huh. Isn't that funny? I thought I was the one who married up, being that Jack is an American hero and all."

A smile flashed across Joe's face.

"Well, I suppose at the end of the day, all women are the same anyway. Trust me Jack, if she's anything like my wife, she'll be laying down house rules before you know it," Chris lamented.

"I only have one house rule, and since all women are alike, I'm sure it's the same rule your wife has," Tess said.

"What's that?" he asked.

"Morning sex. There should always be time for morning sex."

Chris's jaw dropped, along with everyone else's. Jack turned beet red, looked down, and chuckled.

Tess pecked him on the cheek. "Please excuse me, my love. I see that Abdul and Layla have arrived." She walked away, Chris's mouth still agape.

"Oh, you're a lucky man, Jack," Joe said with a laugh.

"Seriously, can you get her to talk to Gina?" Bobby added.

They all clinked their beer bottles.

"I'm gonna go get something to eat. Congrats again," Chris mumbled, slithering away.

As soon as Chris was out of earshot, Joe burst into laughter. "Tess is a pistol, Jack. She doesn't take any crap and she had his number right away."

"She's seriously awesome," Bobby said. "I love her."

"Not as much as I do," Jack said.

***

Tess and Omar walked over with the older couple that had just arrived. "Honey, these are my special friends, Abdul and Layla. This is my husband, Jack, and these are our friends, Joe and Bobby. They all work together."

"Very nice to meet you," Jack said, extending his hand.

"Are you exhausted from your trip?" Tess asked. "They flew in yesterday from Dubai to be here," she told the group.

"We are well rested," Layla said. "Thank you for taking care of the arrangements for us. The flowers in the hotel are spectacular. I can't believe you remembered my favorites."

"It was the least I could do. I couldn't possibly get married without you and Abdul. It was so generous of you to come all this way."

"You're very kind," Abdul said. "We wouldn't have missed it for the world. Anything for you, Tess. You are my light."

Tess blushed. "You know the difficult job that Jack and his friends have. I wanted you to tell them about your work. It's the other side of the same coin. Like me, you see the world in terms of light and dark. I was hoping you could tell them about the light." She turned to the group, "Abdul is Ambassador of the Arts for the United Arab

Emirates. For many years, he's been working to promote peace around the world through the arts."

"That's incredible," Joe said. "Is that how you two met?"

Tess nodded. "Omar told me about what Abdul was trying to achieve and I simply had to meet him."

"When we met, we knew we were kindred spirits," Abdul said. "I always felt that I saw people differently than others do. As a boy, I thought there was something wrong with me, but as I got older, my faith showed me that what I thought was a detriment was actually my path forward. It wasn't until I met Tess that I knew I wasn't alone. She's the first person I've met who sees people as I do. Tess, do you agree?"

"Yes. It was such a relief. For years, I felt misunderstood. People assumed that I must be childlike or naïve to see the world the way I do. They thought I couldn't see the differences between people, as if that were something to aspire to. But when you don't see people's differences, you don't see their humanity or their struggles. How could I write without truly witnessing people?" She paused and lowered her voice. "I see differences, details. But I also see something beyond them. I can hold two thoughts."

Abdul smiled. "Precisely."

"Please tell them about what you do," Tess said.

Abdul proceeded to tell the group about his work. They listened intently, their eyes growing wider as he went on. When he was finished, each one thanked him.

Bobby said, "I had no idea this was going on."

Jack looked bowled over. "I'm so impressed. It restores my faith."

"I told you. It's awe inspiring. He's one of the most incredible human beings I've ever known," Tess said.

Abdul smiled modestly and said, "Tess has not shared her role in this effort."

"I've done nothing," Tess rebuffed. "This is about your work."

Abdul laughed and turned to Omar. "Do you think giving away millions of books is nothing? Do you think that what she has done for the women who read those books, many in secret, is nothing? Tell me

Omar, when she was standing by my side, touring the Middle East against everyone's advice, with all the horrific rape and death threats, refusing the extra security we all knew she needed, did you feel that was nothing? Perhaps my memory fails."

Omar's expression turned serious. "It was terrifying and very real. I begged her not to do it."

Tess looked down.

"Butterfly, it wasn't nothing," Omar said.

Jack, Joe, and Bobby couldn't look away, but knew it was best to keep their mouths shut and listen.

"Do you know what I remember, Abdul?" Tess said.

"Please tell me," he replied.

"How you taught me to transform myself into a vessel, and shield myself in light for protection. I couldn't have survived those years without that skill. Thank you."

Abdul tilted his chin downward. "Knowing who you are in your soul, I always thought it must have been quite difficult for you. Not the people, but all the rest of it, the chatter, as you would say. Tell me, was it difficult?"

"Difficult?" she whispered, a tear trickling down her face. "It was excruciating."

"Why did you do it?"

She wiped her cheek. "You already know the answer. There's only one reason to do anything."

He smiled. "For love."

She nodded.

Jack lightly rubbed her back, tracing his finger down her spine.

"That reminds me of the most harrowing day of our tour," Abdul said. "Do you remember?"

"Of course."

Abdul looked at the group. "There was a mob and no way past them. We were going to miss our next scheduled appearance. Our security team stuck us in a hotel room and told us we needed to cancel our next stop. Tess refused. She ordered them out of the room. You should have seen their faces; they were not used to a woman giving them commands. When they left, she looked me squarely in the eyes and said, 'The only way out is through.' I reluctantly agreed. Tess, do you remember what we did next?"

She smiled.

He took her hands and closed his eyes. "We held hands and quietly chanted, 'There is only darkness and light, and love is the bridge between them.' We repeated those words over and over again. 'There is only darkness and light, and love is the bridge between them.' We opened the door, and the guards asked what we were doing. I'll never forget, Tess said, 'We're leaving. You can come with us or stay here,' and she marched past them." He stopped to laugh.

"What happened next?" Joe asked.

"We passed safely through the crowd," Abdul said.

"Wow. That was very brave, Tess," Joe said.

Tess shook her head. "That's what Abdul thought at the time, too. But now he knows better."

"What do you mean?" Jack asked.

"Not caring what happens to you is not the same as being brave."

Abdul smiled. "But tonight Tess, I see a hint of something in your eyes I've never seen before: fear." He squeezed her hands. "It's wonderful. I'm very happy for you. You must finally feel like you have something to lose."

Two more guests walked through the front door, and Tess said, "Ah, it looks like I'm literally saved by the bell. My friend Mick is here, please excuse me."

She sauntered off. The group looked over to see who was arriving. Their jaws hit the floor. Bobby stammered, "Uh, is that..."

Jack shook his head. "She said one of her friends was a singer."

Abdul smiled. "That's how she sees him. She sees something beyond the details."

***

Tess and Mick walked over to the group, another man trailing behind.

"Abdul and Layla went to get some food," Omar said. He shook Mick's hand. "Great to see you."

"You too, Omar. Tess called, so here I am," Mick said. "I'm just dying to meet the man who landed you, darling. It's rare I meet a man luckier than I am."

She giggled. "This is my husband, Jack."

"I've heard quite a bit about you. You've swept this one off her feet. A pleasure," Mick said, extending his hand.

"So amazing to meet you," Jack said, shaking his hand.

"And these are our friends Bobby and Joe," Tess said.

"Nice to meet you," they all said, starstruck.

"Oh, and this goon behind me is Eddie. They won't let me travel without personal security, an insurance thing," Mick said, rolling his eyes. "I brought what you asked for. Eddie's got it in that tube. Where should he put it?"

"Oh, thank you. He can stick it over there by the door," she said. "Can I get you something to drink?"

"I'll get it, and then we dance," he said, squeezing her hand.

"The bar is set up through there, in the dining room."

"Sparkling water, no fruit for you?" he asked.

"Please."

"I'll be back."

As he walked off, Jack looked at her and said, "He knows what you drink?"

"Well of course, honey. Don't your friends know what you drink?"

He let out an audible huff and smiled.

"I feel like I'm having an out-of-body experience. You know I love their music," Bobby said.

"I remember," Tess replied.

"Butterfly, I see Clay chatting with Abdul and Layla. I'm going to join them unless you need me," Omar said.

"Go, enjoy yourself."

"But if Mick invites us to stay at his place in London again, you have to say yes. Pretty please?"

"I told you, never again."

"But why, Butterfly?"

"Because I'm not nocturnal."

"I know, but it was so much fun."

Tess shook her head. "You're impossible. Go spend time with your handsome man before he has second thoughts about you."

"That was cold, Tess," he said with a smirk.

Omar walked off as Mick returned with drinks. "So Jack, your job is fascinating. Tell me about saving the world," he said.

Jack laughed. They spoke until Mick's glass was empty. He looked at Tess devilishly. "Well darling, shall we dance?"

"Sure," she replied. She rested a hand on Jack's chest. "We always dance."

Mick put his glass down. "But first, I must ask you something. Darling, is your husband a jealous man?"

"He knows he has no reason to be."

Jack blushed.

"Good," Mick said. "Because you know how I dance, and he looks like he could hurt me."

"Honey, my husband could snap your neck before that crossing guard you hired has time to get his hands off the cheese tray."

Jack nearly spit out his drink. Everyone held their laughter until Mick burst into hysterics. "Oh, darling, I've missed you." He hollered, "Eddie, get your grubby hands off the brie!"

"Ha! That's the line of the night. It's even better than 'There's not enough meat on this deli platter.' They really should leave these things to the professionals," Tess said.

Mick laughed.

"You've seen *Spinal Tap*?" Bobby asked.

"Of course," Tess said.

"What's *Spinal Tap*?" Jack asked.

"It's a mock documentary about a rock band. It's kind of the worst and best thing ever," Bobby said.

"Totally," Tess said. "And since you've never seen it, Jack, I know what we'll be doing tomorrow."

Mick took Tess's hand. "Shall we dance?"

"After you." She followed him, looked over her shoulder, and winked at Jack.

***

Later in the evening, Tess was sitting in the corner chatting with Mick and her hairdresser, Denise. Mick got up and strolled over to Omar, Jack, Joe, and Bobby.

"That Denise is quite a girl," Mick said. "Tess always had the coolest friends. Jack, let's have some fun with your new bride. Omar, can you play a certain song?"

"Oh, I know what you're thinking. She'll be cross with me," Omar said.

Mick laughed. "Let's fill Jack and his friends in."

They listened eagerly.

"Tess threw a party several years ago in LA," Omar said. "She had a gorgeous yard, the whole thing illuminated with twinkly lights."

"And she was wearing this fabulous long, flowy white dress. It was impossibly LA," Mick added. "Anyway, Elton's 'Tiny Dancer' came on and a few of us noticed Tess started to dance. She was actually twirling about like a ballerina. It was glorious. We loved watching her so much that we didn't want it to end. Someone had the idea to put it on repeat. Who was that?" Mick asked.

"It was Ronnie," Omar said.

"Yes! The rascal!" Mick exclaimed. "So, we put the song on repeat. Tess danced to it four or five times before she noticed. When she finally realized, she got so hysterical she collapsed into a heap on the grass. It was magnificent."

The men all belly laughed.

"Omar, go put it on," Mick directed.

Omar shook his head and said, "You're taking the heat for this one," before he headed off to change the music.

"It's the pre-chorus," Mick said. "I guarantee that she'll start moving, like she can't help it. Then when the chorus comes, *bang*."

Omar returned a moment later, just as the song began to play.

As if pulled by an invisible string, Tess stood up. "Here we go," Mick said. Soon, she was twirling in the corner as if no one was there, as promised. Jack was beaming. Mick and Omar started cackling so loudly that it drew Tess's attention. Her mouth flew open and she started shaking her head and laughing. She flipped them the middle finger and just continued dancing. They all laughed so hard they could hardly stand.

"High priestess of pain, my ass," Mick said. "That girl is a ray of light."

"What are you talking about?" Jack asked.

"Some asshole reviewer. He had her all wrong," Mick replied.

Omar said, "After her third novel came out, a reviewer wrote a story titled 'The People's High Priestess of Pain Is Back at It.' It gutted her. Everyone else called her inspirational and the book 'a breath of fresh air,' but that label stuck and it's all she remembered. It wasn't the review. She doesn't give a shit about that. It was what the words meant. She wears those words like a scarlet letter."

Jack turned his attention back to Tess, still dancing as if only she could hear the music.

**

At the end of the night, only a couple of their closest friends remained. As they were saying goodbye to Bobby and Gina, Tess grabbed the cardboard tube by the door.

"Here, Mick brought this for you," she said, handing it to Bobby.

"For me?" he asked in disbelief.

"It's a poster signed by the whole band. One of their songs came on at the bar once, and you mentioned they were your favorite group."

"Are you serious? I don't know what to say. That's... unbelievable!" he stammered. He turned to Gina, "Oh my God, is this the coolest thing ever, or what?" He turned back to Tess. "Thank you so much," he said, hugging her. "Congratulations again, you guys."

After they left, Omar said, "Okay, Tiny Dancer, that's a wrap."

"I'm gonna get you for that," she warned.

Omar smiled. "You two should get to bed. Clay and I will make sure the caterers finish the cleanup. We'll let ourselves out and lock up when everyone is gone."

Tess hugged him. "Thank you. I love you."

"I'm so happy for you, Butterfly."

"Thank you," Jack said, shaking his hand. "Good night, Clay."

"Oh, if you two didn't get any wedding cake, there's still some left," Omar said.

"Let's grab a piece," Jack said.

"I don't eat cake," Tess replied.

"Maybe you'll want a bite," he said.

On their way to the bedroom, they stopped in the dining room and picked up a piece of vanilla cake slathered in white frosting. When they got to their room at long last, Jack shut the door and Tess flicked off her shoes.

"Hey, come here Mrs. Miller," Jack said.

"I like the sound of that."

He wove his fingers into her hair and kissed her. "Did you have fun tonight?"

"Oodles, but I couldn't wait to be alone with you. Did your friends have a good time?"

"Yeah. I think you made Bobby's whole life. That was really sweet."

"It was nothing."

Jack let out a puff and smiled. "You would say that."

She shrugged.

"I think the best part of the night was what you said to Chris. His mouth is probably still hanging open. I can't believe you said that."

"Actually, I thought I was quite reserved. I wanted to say blow jobs."

He laughed.

"That guy is kind of a prick."

Jack smiled and picked up the piece of cake with his hand. "Would you like a bite, Mrs. Miller?"

She nodded and he held the cake up to her. She took a small bite, letting in the sweetness.

CHAPTER 9

The days, weeks, and months passed after their wedding. Tess and Jack loved each other more each day. Jack learned that when Tess was immersed in writing, she could be chained to her laptop for twelve hours straight. She didn't like missing time with him, so he would bring a newspaper or an iPad with headphones into her office and sit patiently in the corner. After months of wedded bliss, Jack noticed that Tess was no longer counting out every morsel of food, but would casually toss a handful of nuts or granola into a bowl.

Tess learned that Jack considered every security threat that came across his desk to be his personal responsibility to thwart. On the days when this was impossible, he would come home with the weight of the world heavy on his shoulders. Instead of burying the hard days and dark feelings, he began to walk through them, safe and secure in her love.

Jack was hugely protective of Tess. He learned where to seat her in restaurants or bars so that she would have privacy, and he became attuned to the look in people's eyes when they recognized her. He could immediately tell by her demeanor whether to allow someone to approach her. There were times he wrestled with his desire to defend Tess and he had to force himself to consider her disdain for violence.

One day, they were strolling through a museum when Jack noticed a couple of guys staring at Tess. She started pulling Jack in another direction, so he knew she wanted to steer clear. Sure enough, they quickly approached Tess, one of them saying, "Aren't you that writer? You're worth like a billion dollars."

Tess held Jack's hand, keeping her other hand in her pocket. She smiled at them and tried to walk away.

The guy hollered, "You don't have to be a bitch."

Jack spun around, his face red. "What did you say?" he yelled.

"Jack, please, just ignore them. Please," Tess begged.

He looked at the guys and said, "Don't ever speak to a woman that way."

They walked away.

"Thank you for not escalating it," Tess said.

"I wanted to pummel him," Jack said.

"If you do that every time some jerk says something to me, it's going to be a very long and very violent life. It's okay to let it go, baby. Jack…"

"Yeah?"

They stopped walking and she looked him in the eyes. "I would never want you to harm someone else for my sake. The only darkness that frightens me is in you."

He was stunned. "You're not scared of me?"

"Of course not. But sometimes I'm scared *for* you. It's your soul I care about, not guys like that."

Another night, Tess and Gina met Jack and Bobby at a bar. The women arrived first. When Jack and Bobby walked in, two men were hassling them. "We told you, no thank you," Gina said to one of the guys. The other guy touched Tess's shoulder, and Jack and Bobby tore across the room to them.

Jack grabbed the guy's shoulders and screamed, "Don't touch her or you'll have to deal with me."

"Get the fuck out of here. Now!" Bobby said.

When they sat down at the table, Tess looked at Jack and said, "You know, men try to pick up women sometimes. You might have overreacted."

"He touched you. I wanted to slam his head into the bar," Jack said.

"Well then, I guess your reaction wasn't that bad," she joked.

He looked upset. She brushed the side of his face. "It's okay. Just try to take a beat."

Then there was the scariest incident of all. It was a Friday night at Shelby's Bar, and Tess, Jack, Joe, and Bobby were sitting at their usual table having a drink. Gina was at home with a cold, Clay was on call at the hospital, and Omar was running late. A man walked into the bar and Tess clenched Jack's hand and muttered, "I don't believe it."

"What is it?" he asked.

"I hope that man doesn't come over here," she replied.

"Who is he?" Jack asked.

"Arlo Mathers. He's a publisher. Let's just say he has very poor manners with women."

"We've got you," Bobby said.

Joe nodded. "Absolutely."

Arlo moseyed up to the table. "Tess Lee, I can't believe it," he said.

Tess didn't respond.

"I'm in town for a conference and stopped for a drink," he said.

"Congratulations," Tess replied.

He snorted. "Tess, may I please speak with you privately? I'd love to clear the air."

"I have nothing to say to you. Please leave. In fact, go get a drink somewhere else," she replied.

"But Tess, I…"

Jack stood up. "She asked you to leave."

He snorted again. "Tess, you never looked better," he said, walking away from the table and out the door.

Jack sat down and put his arm around Tess. "You okay, baby?"

She nodded. "Thank you for getting rid of him. Let's talk about something else."

Bobby started talking about all of Gina's plans for the wedding. Inspired by Tess and Jack's happiness, Bobby had finally proposed, and now his weekends consisted of meetings with photographers and florists. Half an hour later, Omar arrived. "I'm so sorry I'm late. Butterfly, Larry is about to board his jet for Tokyo and there are some questions about the giving statement in the end credits. It would be fastest if you just called him. Pretty please?"

"Sure thing. Excuse me, gentleman. I'll be right back."

As Tess walked out, Omar raised his hand, signaling the waitress for a beer. He grabbed a handful of pretzels and started gobbling on them. "Insane day, I can't remember when I last ate something."

"Omar, who's Arlo Mathers?" Jack asked.

"Well, that's a name I hoped to never hear again. He's in publishing. Reprehensible guy. Tess had a bad feeling about him from the moment they met. Her instincts are always spot-on," Omar replied. The waitress delivered his beer and he took a swig.

"Tess said he has poor manners with women," Jack said.

"Ha! That's like saying Charles Manson is impolite. Another good thing that came from getting her out of LA is that she's far away from that sexual predator. I'm telling you, he was obsessed. I still don't understand how he managed to lure her out of that charity soiree. Thank God those men found her in time. It took both of them to pull him off her. She should have pressed charges; she had bruises on her wrists for weeks. But you know how she is, never thinks of herself, didn't want to risk harming the charity. Why are we talking about this asshole?"

Jack started shaking. "He was here tonight. He came up to the table and asked Tess to speak with him."

"Arlo Mathers was here?" Omar said. His face fell. "I just asked Tess to go outside by herself."

Jack leapt from the table, the three other men following close behind. They raced outside. Tess was leaning against the building and Arlo was standing in front of her, his arm against the brick exterior, blocking her in. Jack flew over, grabbed him, and punched him. He fell to the ground, blood spewing from his broken nose. Jack leaned down for another go at him, but Bobby grabbed him from behind. "He isn't worth it," Bobby said. "Do you really want Tess to see this?"

Jack stood over him, his chest heaving. Then he looked over at Tess, hunched over, her face in her hands. "It's okay, baby. You're okay." He took her in his arms and rubbed her head. "Why didn't you tell me?"

"Because I love you more than I hate him."

Tess was equally protective of Jack. She hated how hard he was on himself. When he was dealing with a national security crisis or some terrorist threat, he would come home at all hours of the night, his eyes glazed from having faced the worst of humanity. Tess would curl up beside him, silently running her fingers along his body until she could feel him let the darkness go. One day, there was a suicide bombing in DC with several civilian casualties. Tess had spoken on the phone with Jack amidst the chaos, and he said, "It's my fault. I couldn't stop them in time." Tess waited in the living room until he finally came home at four in the morning. She brushed his face with the back of her hand and then started taking his clothes off. They made love on the couch. They held each other and she whispered, "It isn't your fault. You did everything you could." They grabbed leftover Chinese food from the refrigerator and ate it cold out of the containers, wrapped in a throw blanket on the couch.

They often passed little girls on the street or strolling through the park, and Jack would lower his head ever so slightly. Tess would intertwine her fingers with his, pull him close, and whisper, "The only way out is through. Just feel it." He'd wipe tears from his eyes. On those days, Tess always remembered to ask him to tell her more about Gracie. Over time, she could see that while the pain remained, he was also learning how to feel the love. One day, he brought her up out of the blue. They were reading the Sunday newspaper and he flipped past the comics and said, "Gracie loved comics." Tess smiled.

Then there were the times someone would give him grief, and in turn, Tess would give them hell. Once, she picked up Jack at his office for lunch. He was sitting in his office with Joe and Chris, deep in concentration, but broke into a huge smile when she appeared in his doorway. "Hi, sweetheart."

She greeted Joe and Chris and then said, "I can wait outside while you finish up, honey."

Chris said, "Jack, are you going somewhere?"

"Tess and I are stepping out for lunch. We can wrap this up when I get back," he replied.

Chris turned to Tess. "Do you really think it's responsible for Jack to leave in the middle of the day?"

Joe looked down and shook his head.

Jack opened his mouth to speak, but Tess jumped in. She stared Chris down and said, "I realize our national security might require the total sacrifice of a few soulless robots, and for this, the citizens of our country thank you. However, you might want to spend some quality time with your wife before you have the gall to insinuate that my husband is irresponsible." Then she walked over to Joe, kissed him on the cheek, and said, "Always a pleasure to see you." She turned to Jack and said, "I'll be right outside, honey."

When she left the room, Joe burst into laughter. Jack shook his head.

"Tess really doesn't like me," Chris said.

"It's a real mystery," Joe said, wiping the tears from his eyes. Jack chuckled.

Tess and Jack also enjoyed spending time with their friends. They spent many evenings together, laughing uproariously. One night at the bar, they were sharing their most embarrassing or entertaining stories. Bobby told them a hilarious story from his time in the academy. Jack nudged Tess and said, "Your turn."

"Hmm. I don't know," she replied.

"Oh, I do," Omar said gleefully. "Jack, you're going to love this. We were at a gala in London where Tess was being honored..."

Tess interrupted. "I know where this is going and you're not telling that story," she said, picking up a pretzel and flinging it at his head.

"Butterfly, I'll wear that basket as a hat, but I am telling the story," he said, grinning like a Cheshire cat.

"Fine, but I'm making two objections. First, I wasn't embarrassed."

"I know, but you should have been," Omar said, chucking a pretzel back at her. "But that's all right, I was embarrassed enough for the both of us."

She shook her head. "Second, it's not that funny."

"If by 'not that funny' you mean it's epically funny, then you'd be right," he said with a chuckle. "In fact, it may be the funniest story to ever happen to anyone."

She tossed another pretzel at him, but he dodged it.

"This must be good," Bobby said.

"Go on, Omar," Joe urged.

"You're all terrible," Tess protested, looking to Jack for support.

"Don't look at me, I want to hear it," Jack said.

She rolled her eyes. "Fine, but my objections stand." She crossed her arms and put on an exaggerated pout.

"Duly noted, Butterfly. So, Tess was in London, receiving an award for her humanitarian efforts in the arts."

"Such a ridiculous thing to receive an award for," Tess interjected.

"Nice attempt at deflection, Butterfly. You can give us a diatribe about the absurdity of awards another time," Omar said.

Tess rolled her eyes.

"Another of the honorees was…"

"Don't you say his name," Tess said.

"Let's just say he was in the greatest band of all time."

"You don't mean?" Bobby said.

"Yes, Paul himself," Omar replied. "Anyway, after the award ceremony, Paul was hosting a little party at his place and he invited us. He had just purchased a Picasso at auction for something crazy like thirty million dollars and he wanted Tess's opinion. You have to remember that she had just been honored as a literary genius and artistic visionary. So, Paul and all his guests stood around waiting to hear her profound words of wisdom. What does Tess do? She looks at the painting, cocks her head, and says, 'Peekaboo, why so blue?'"

They all cracked up.

"You did not say that!" Jack said through fits of laughter.

"I did," Tess said, turning red.

"Peekaboo, why so blue? What does that even mean?" Bobby asked.

Tess shrugged. "I have no idea; it's just what came out. The whole situation was so absurd."

"What did Paul do?" Joe asked.

"Well, that's the best part of the story. At first, everyone just stood there in a state of shock. After a moment passed, Paul said, 'Too right, Tess. Peekaboo, why so blue?' as if she was some kind of genius. Everyone started clapping over this great insight," Omar said, now hysterical.

Everyone laughed so hard they were falling off their chairs.

"I still don't think it's that funny," Tess protested.

Try as he might, Jack was unable to stop laughing.

Omar finally composed himself and said, "Now, every time Paul wants to buy a piece of art, I mean even a bloody poster for his bathroom, he FaceTimes Tess to get her opinion."

They all laughed so hard they were holding their stomachs.

"He FaceTimes you?" Jack asked when he could get the words out.

"Not often," Tess replied.

"When was the last time?" Omar asked.

"About four months ago," Tess replied.

Omar raised his eyebrows. "And, what did he want?"

Tess looked down sheepishly. "He was trying to choose between two Tiffany lamps and he wanted my opinion."

Everyone got so hysterical they could hardly breathe. Even Tess was laughing now.

"She's like his art oracle," Omar squealed.

Jack pulled Tess to him. "You're supposed to be on my side," she said. "It's not that funny."

"I'm always on your side, but sweetheart, it *is* that funny."

Through all these moments, Tess and Jack had each other's backs and their bond grew. Soon the months had turned into a year. Tess released a new novel, which she loved writing but declined to promote. At Jack's suggestion, she pre-signed ten thousand copies for her publisher, giving fans a chance to buy autographed copies. Jack learned to look to Tess in his dark or dour moments, take a beat, and breathe. With Tess's help, he found ways to let the darkness go. And Friday nights with their friends grew into a series of game nights and potlucks at each other's homes, in addition to evenings at Shelby's Bar.

CHAPTER 10

When Jack's alarm went off that Wednesday morning, Tess jumped up. "Let me run in to brush my teeth."

He yawned.

Soon, Tess returned to the bedroom wearing a black lace teddy. She sashayed to Jack's side of the bed. "Good morning, Mr. Miller."

He reached out and caressed her leg. "What's going on here? I have work, baby. You're going to make me late again."

"I'm simply enforcing the house codes. You can be ten minutes late."

He smiled. "Okay, wait for me." He darted to the bathroom.

When he returned, Tess was kneeling at the edge of the bed. He walked over and started kissing her. He paused long enough to say, "I can be twenty minutes late."

After making love, they lay in bed touching each other's faces. "You know, I think I owe Chris one. If he hadn't been such a prick at our wedding, you may not have created such a great house rule. We have the best mornings."

Tess giggled. "We do. And the best nights."

Jack kissed her. "I'm so late."

"I know. Go get ready. I'll make you a coffee to go."

"Thank you," he said, kissing her one more time before slipping out of bed.

Fifteen minutes later, Jack whizzed into the kitchen, clean and dressed. "That was record timing. Here," Tess said, handing him a to-go tumbler and something wrapped in foil. "I fixed you coffee and a bagel."

"Thank you, sweetheart."

"I'm going to the library today to do research for my book. I'll stop at the store afterward to pick up something for dinner. Any special requests?"

"Whatever you want," he said. He leaned in for a quick peck. "I love you."

"I love you, too. Have a great day," she said, smiling widely.

***

Just past noon, Jack was reviewing a file with Joe when his cell phone rang.

"Miller here," he answered.

"Mr. Miller, this is Vivian, your housecleaner."

"Yes?"

"Something is wrong with Mrs. Miller, and I think you should come home right away."

"What happened?" he asked, panic in his voice.

"I don't know. When I arrived at your home, her phone was smashed in the kitchen and she was sitting in the living room. I could see something was terribly wrong. She said she wasn't safe, and then she ran and hid in the bedroom closet. She's in there now."

"Please don't leave her. I'm on my way," he said. He sprang up and raced out of the room.

Joe called after him. "What's going on?"

"Something happened to Tess," he screamed.

He flew out of the parking garage, speeding toward his house, honking for other cars to move out of the way as he zoomed through every red light. He called Omar on the way.

"Hello?"

"It's Jack. Something's wrong with Tess. The cleaner called and said she's hiding in a closet. I'm on my way now."

"I'll meet you there," Omar said.

When Jack arrived at the house, he surveyed the scene: Tess's destroyed phone was on the kitchen counter, there was an open bottle of vodka and several packs of cigarettes strewn on the coffee table, and the house stank of stale smoke. He dashed into the bedroom. Vivian was standing at the closet door. "Move," he commanded.

Tess was curled up in a ball, cowering in the corner, her hair covering her face. He slid on the floor in front of her. "Tess, it's okay. I'm here," he said tenderly, reaching out to touch her.

She flinched and tried to pull herself further into the corner.

"Sweetheart, it's Jack. It's your Jack," he said.

Her head remained lowered, her arms against her chest.

He reached his hand out and gently touched her shoulder, but she jerked away.

"Okay, it's okay. You just sit there for a minute," he said.

He slowly got up and stepped out of the closet. He looked at Vivian. "Tell me everything that happened from the second you got here."

"I let myself in like always. I noticed her broken phone right away. I saw she was sitting on the couch in the living room, which startled me because she's usually out or upstairs in her office. I apologized for barging in, but she didn't respond so I walked over. She was smoking, which I've never seen her do before. She was trembling and wouldn't look at me so I bent down and said, 'Ms. Lee, is everything all right?' She quietly said, 'Mrs. Miller. My name is Mrs. Miller.' I said, 'I'm sorry. Mrs. Miller, is there something I can do to help you?' She stared blankly ahead and just kept saying, 'I'm not safe. I'm not safe.' Then she ran to the bedroom, got in the closet, and started mumbling 'I'm not safe' again. Eventually, she stopped talking altogether. I told her I was going to call you and she didn't respond. She's been like this ever since."

Just then, Omar arrived. "Jack, what's going on?" he asked, his face flushed.

Jack pointed to the closet. Omar peeked in.

"What happened?"

"I don't know," Jack said, gripping his head with hands.

"It's okay. We'll take care of her," Omar said. Then he gestured to Vivian. "Did she tell you what she knows?"

"Yeah."

"Thank you, Vivian, I think it would be best if you leave now," Omar said.

Vivian nodded and left.

Omar put his hand on Jack's shoulder. "I need you to stay calm and tell me everything that happened today. Don't leave anything out."

Jack took a breath and steadied himself. "We had sex this morning."

"And she was all right?" Omar asked.

Jack's eyes started to tear. "Yes, she was perfect. Then I got ready for work and she fixed me breakfast to take with me. Before I left, she was talking about going to the library and she asked what I wanted for dinner. She was so happy."

"Go on," Omar encouraged.

"The cleaner called just after noon. I raced home and found Tess's phone smashed in the kitchen and Tess was like this. She'd been drinking, Omar."

"It's okay. She's not an alcoholic; that's not why she doesn't drink. What did Vivian say?"

"She said Tess was sitting on the couch, trembling. She asked if she could help her. She called her Ms. Lee and Tess said her name was Mrs. Miller. Then she said she wasn't safe and came in here. She repeated she wasn't safe for a little while and then stopped. I tried to tell her I was here and to comfort her, but she wouldn't even let me touch her. She recoiled when I tried," he said, now getting hysterical. "I haven't even seen her face. I don't know if someone hurt her. Omar, please help her."

Omar nodded and slowly stepped into the closet. He sat on the floor in front of Tess. "Butterfly, it's me, Omar. You're safe now. Jack and I are both here. Everything is okay. I need to know if you understand me. Jack said you don't want anyone to touch you. That's fine. But I need you to look at me so I know that you understand what I'm saying. Can you do that, Butterfly? Can you please look at me?" He waited patiently for a moment and Tess raised her head and looked at him. Omar smiled. "Thank you. Now let's get you somewhere more comfortable. Do you want to lie down in your bed?" She shook her head so slightly it was almost imperceptible. "That's okay. Do you want to go have a seat on the couch, where you were earlier?" She nodded faintly. "I'm going to get up now. You can follow me." He stood up slowly and walked out of the closet. He gestured for Jack to step back. Omar peeked into the closet. "Are you ready?" Tess stood up, her shoulders slumped. She walked to the living room and sat down on the couch, with Omar and Jack following behind her.

"Jack, please get her a glass of water."

Omar sat on the chair adjacent to Tess, observing. There was a plate with several cigarette butts and an open vodka bottle missing a couple of shots. Tess reached for a cigarette and the lighter. She lit the cigarette with shaking hands, exhaling lines of smoke. Jack returned with the water. Omar placed the glass in front of Tess. "Try to take a few sips of water, please," he said. "I'm going to speak with Jack for a minute. We'll be right in the kitchen if you need us."

Tess continued puffing on her cigarette.

Omar and Jack huddled in the kitchen.

"Have you ever seen her like this before?" Jack asked.

"No, never. This is what I think: there are no signs that anyone physically hurt her today. I think she received a phone call from someone who has hurt her or someone she's terrified will hurt her. She's not a fearful person, so it's something real."

"That Arlo guy?" Jack asked.

"I doubt it. Tess isn't scared of him and this runs deeper," Omar replied.

"The men who assaulted her when she was a girl?"

"They're both dead, Jack. But I think whoever called has wounded her deeply and now she's having a significant post-traumatic stress response. We need to try to find out where her last call came from."

"I'll call Bobby. He can find out."

"In the meantime, I need you to try to see the positive here."

He let out a small noise. "There's something positive?"

"Yes. What we are witnessing takes tremendous strength. When this happened, her first reaction was to numb herself; that's why she's drinking and smoking. It wasn't enough to block out the trauma, so she's gone into this protective state. She's protecting herself from something so painful or frightening that she isn't yet able to deal with it. Jack, she didn't try to hurt herself. I believe she's trying to heal herself. She's responsive when I speak to her and in control of her body, and those are good things."

"She won't let me touch her," Jack said, his eyes welling with tears again. "She flinched when I tried. She won't even look at me."

"It's because she loves you more than anything. You can see straight through her. She needs to hide right now, and she can't do that with you. Believe me, when she's ready, you'll be the one she looks for. I'm certain."

Jack sniffled. "How can we help her?"

"For a number of reasons I think the best thing we can do is to try to deal with it here in her home. I'm trained for this and I know her. I can do this, but you should be prepared for her to be like this for many hours or days. I need to know if you're up for it."

"Yes. What do we do?"

"The idea is to let her choose to come back to us, not to force her. She's a sexual assault survivor and it's clear she doesn't want to be touched, so we should honor that. You should stay near her, because it will bring her comfort, but you shouldn't try to force her to look at you. We should speak in quiet tones, nothing jarring. Also, and please don't be alarmed, but I don't want her alone other than to use the bathroom, and even then, you should stand right outside the door. We need to get rid of anything she could use to harm herself: razors, scissors, knives, pills. If you have a gun, secure it."

Jack looked down, his breath labored.

"It's just a precaution. Even after everything that's happened to her in her life, she's never tried to hurt herself, including today. We just need to be careful."

Jack nodded. "What about the cigarettes and vodka?"

"Leave them. They're comforting her and I don't want to take that away. I'm going to call Clay and ask him to drop off some clothes and a toothbrush later tonight. I'll stay here as long as it takes, until she's one hundred percent back to her normal self and we've dealt with whatever or whoever caused this."

"Thank you," Jack said. "I'm so grateful we have you, Omar."

"I promise, I will get you both through this. Do you have Ibuprofen or something? She's been drinking, and most likely on an empty stomach. I want to try to get her to take something so she doesn't end up with a terrible headache."

"Above the kitchen sink."

"I'll try to get her to take them and then I'll see if I can get her to eat something. While I'm doing that, you can go put all those items we discussed out of reach. You might as well change into something more comfortable, too."

Jack nodded and set off.

Omar retrieved Ibuprofen for Tess and sat down in the chair near her. "Please take these and a good drink of water or you'll get a bad headache, Butterfly," he said, placing the pills beside her water.

She picked up the pills and swallowed them, taking several sips from her glass. Then she lay down on the couch, flat on her back, staring at the ceiling. Jack returned ten minutes later in sweats. "It's taken care of and I made a couple of phone calls," he said.

"I think Tess wants to rest. Where can I find a blanket for her?" Omar asked.

"The upstairs hall closet," Jack said.

Omar got up and Jack sat in the chair on the other side of the room, where he had a clear view of her face. The distress was gone from her eyes, but now they were completely vacant. When Omar returned, he held the blanket in front of Tess. "Do you want this?"

She took the blanket, unfurled it over her body, turned to the inside of the couch, and shut her eyes. Jack and Omar stayed with Tess until she woke up four hours later.

When she finally woke from her nap, she got up and walked toward her bedroom without a word. Jack followed her. She walked into the bathroom, shutting the door behind her. He stood on the other side of the door, counting the seconds, terrified of her being out of sight. He heard the toilet flush and the faucet turn on and off. A moment later, she opened the door and returned to the couch.

Omar served her scrambled eggs and asked her to "please eat." She didn't touch them, and instead smoked half a dozen cigarettes before lying back down, staring at the ceiling. Soon, Bobby called Jack to report that Tess's last phone call came from a public phone in a hospital in Rhode Island. There was no way to know who made the call, and Omar couldn't make any sense of it. Clay dropped off a bag for Omar, and at eleven o'clock that night, he settled in to one of the guest rooms, advising Jack to wake him immediately if anything changed. Tess lay awake all night, just looking at the ceiling. Jack sat in the chair watching her.

***

Omar emerged just after dawn and came to check on them. "Good morning, Butterfly," he said with a sweet smile, and then he walked into the kitchen with Jack following behind. "No change?" he asked.

"She's been like that all night," Jack replied.

"Did you get any sleep?"

Jack shook his head. "You?"

"Barely, I'm trying to keep it together to get you both through this, but it's torture seeing her like this. Let's have a shift change. Go take a shower."

"I don't want to leave her," Jack said.

"I'll sit with her. It won't do her any good if you're a mess when she needs you. Take a shower and shave. Then I want her to shower and brush her teeth. She needs to have some sense of routine. You can set out a towel and some fresh clothes for her. We need to give her privacy, but I also don't want her unsupervised. Leave the bathroom door ajar while she showers and stand outside of it. Don't look and don't speak to her, unless she asks for you. Once she's done, I'll try to get her to eat some breakfast. Getting something solid into her would help her chemistry enormously. Okay?"

Jack nodded. "Yeah, okay."

He returned fifteen minutes later, looking less disheveled but still deeply troubled and exhausted. Tess was sitting up on the couch.

"Butterfly, you need to brush your teeth and take a shower. Please get up and go. Jack will make sure you have everything you need."

She didn't move.

"Butterfly, you'll feel better if you shower and change into fresh pajamas. Please."

She got up and walked to the bathroom, Jack following behind. He pointed to a folded towel on the counter and fresh clothes beside it. "Those are for you. There's one of those hair things on top; I know you don't like to get your hair wet in the shower." He turned on the shower and tested the temperature until it was just right. "Sweetheart, I'll be right outside the door if you need anything."

He left the room and leaned against the wall just outside the door. Tess brushed her teeth and showered. When she was done, she opened the bathroom door and Jack stepped aside. She walked into the kitchen where Omar was waiting. He pulled out a barstool.

"I made you coffee, juice, and oatmeal. Please take a seat."

She sat down and picked up the coffee. She took a sip and then slid off the stool and returned to the couch. She lit a cigarette and slowly drank the coffee. Omar brought the juice and oatmeal to her. "Please try to have a little, Butterfly. You need something in your stomach." She didn't touch them. When she was done with the coffee, she put the mug down and lay on her back, shutting her eyes.

Jack walked calmly to the kitchen, and when he was out of Tess's sight, he started crying, holding his head and rocking back and forth. Omar came and put his hands on Jack's shoulders. "I know it's difficult. It's killing me too, more than you know. I promise you that she will be okay. She won't be like this forever."

"When my daughter was sick, when she died, I felt so powerless. I never thought I could feel that helpless again. And now this is happening to Tess, my Tess," he sobbed. "I can't lose her. I would do anything to make everything all right."

Omar rubbed his back. "You are. You are doing more than you know."

Jack stood up, wiped his face, and caught his breath. "We shouldn't leave her alone."

A couple of hours later, Omar tried to get Tess to eat something, but she refused again. In the afternoon, he had an idea and motioned to Jack.

"Do you think you could get Bobby to come over here?" Omar asked.

"Yes. He and Joe have both been texting and offering to come help, but I didn't think we should let anyone near her."

"She must be starving and dehydrated. At this point, food is what would help her the most, but it's not something we can force.

Neither of us are able to get her to eat, so I think we need to get someone else in here with lighter energy to try. Bobby has the right demeanor and she really likes him."

"I'll call him," Jack said.

"Okay. I'll let him know exactly what to do."

***

An hour later, Bobby arrived holding two plastic bags.

"Thanks for coming," Jack said.

"Of course. Anything for you and Tess. How's she doing?"

Jack's expression was pained. "She hasn't spoken or eaten in thirty hours. She's lying on the couch."

Bobby glanced over. "I'm so sorry. Hopefully this will help. Here, I picked up some sandwiches for you guys. I figured you could use something to eat. How are you holding up, Jack?"

"I'm a wreck. Just please try to get her to eat."

"Omar, is there anything I should know that you didn't tell me over the phone?" Bobby asked.

"Try to talk to her normally. She'll be unresponsive, but talk anyway. She feels comfortable with you, so be yourself. Don't touch her or get too close. Keep it light and easy," Omar said.

"Got it."

Bobby walked into the living room. "Hey, Tess. I brought some food," he said, placing the bag on the coffee table.

She rolled onto her side to face him. He opened the bag and took out two bottles of water, two tubs of soup, and a box of crackers. He opened the waters and placed one in front of her. Then he took napkins, plastic spoons, and a paper plate out of the bag. "I got us tomato soup. It's always been one of my favorites, and Omar said that's what you like," he said, removing the lid from her container. "It might be hot though, so we should let it cool off." Then he put the paper plate in the middle of the table, opened the box of crackers, and spilled some onto the plate. "Jack said these are your favorites. The box says they're made with cassava. I have no idea what that is, but it sounds healthy. Gina's always trying to get me to eat healthier. She says I can't live on burgers and chicken wings."

Tess sat up, facing him, her legs curled up in front of her body.

Jack and Omar were standing in the kitchen with bated breath.

"Anyway, I'm curious to try these," Bobby said, picking up a few crackers. He popped one in his mouth. "Hey, you're right. These are really good. Want some?" he asked, pushing the paper plate closer to her.

She reached over, picked up a cracker, and ate it.

"I dig 'em," Bobby said, picking up a handful and eating them one by one. "Anyway, the thing is that I'm not really a good cook. It makes it a lot harder to eat healthy."

Tess reached over and picked up a handful of crackers, sat back, and ate them as he spoke.

Omar put his hand on Jack's shoulder and whispered, "He's so good. I knew this would work."

Jack nodded and sniffled, tears in his eyes.

"Gina is a pretty good cook, but she's always busy so we end up getting a lot of takeout. Jack told me you're a great cook, but he did tell me a funny story about a time you made him muffins. He said you forgot an ingredient or something and they didn't rise. He said they were like hockey pucks, but you were so disappointed and he felt so badly for you that he ate them anyway. Jack's always doing things like that. He's such a good guy and he loves you so much."

Tess finished her crackers and took a few sips of water.

"You know, the soup is probably cool enough by now," Bobby said, picking up his container. He ate a spoonful. "Mmm, this is really good."

Tess picked up her soup and began eating. Jack had to turn away, tears streaming down his face.

"You know, since you're the one who helped me pick out Gina's engagement ring, I have to confess that I'm a little nervous. Don't get me wrong, I know she's the one. I can't wait to marry her. But I'm a little worried about living together. I've never lived with anyone before and I don't want to get on her nerves. Jack told me that you two have never had a fight. I told him I didn't understand how two people could live together for a year and never argue. He told me you said there's no reason to ever argue because you love each other and everything else is just details to sort out. I thought that was really beautiful. I hope Gina and I can be like that."

They both continued eating.

"After I proposed, Gina said she hopes we can be half as happy as you and Jack. Everyone feels that way. What you two have is so special. Jack hasn't been the same since he met you, in the best way. I used to feel kind of bad for him. I mean, he's the nicest, most loyal guy in the world, and he gave everything to his job and his country, and I always felt badly that he didn't really have a life beyond that. You gave him a life. You mean everything to him. I'm sure you know that, but I just wanted to tell you. Anyway, we're going to start looking at apartments soon. Finally buying something. Gina was hoping you could help us. You have such great taste. Honestly, I think she just wants you there to gang up on me. If we don't see eye to eye, I think she wants you to be the tiebreaker. Honestly, it's fine with me. Whatever she wants."

Tess put her container down. It was empty. She lay down, facing Bobby.

"It was great to see you, Tess. Thanks for listening. I'm gonna clean this stuff up. I'll leave the crackers here in case you want more," Bobby said, picking up the containers and spoons.

He walked into the kitchen and quietly said, "Man, I'm so sorry Jack. It was hard to imagine what shape she was in until I saw her with my own eyes."

"That was the best thing that's happened here in thirty hours. Thank you," Jack said. He cleared his throat and continued, "She won't even look at me."

"Jack, I told you why," Omar said. "It's because she loves you more than anyone and she's just not ready yet."

Bobby nodded. "Every time I said your name, her eyes changed. I'm no expert, but after what I just saw, I agree with Omar."

"I hope so," Jack said.

"I was right about Bobby and I'm right about this. Please, I know how difficult it is, but you have to trust me."

Jack nodded.

"She's so sweet, it guts me to think of someone hurting her. I can't imagine how you feel," Bobby said.

"When I find out who did this to her, I'm going to kill him," Jack said.

***

Tess lay on the couch all night, and Jack sat in a chair watching her. Omar stumbled into the kitchen in the morning and waved Jack over.

"Why don't you go take a shower? I'll sit with her. Then you can help her like you did yesterday. I'll make her some breakfast and try to get her to talk."

Jack nodded.

When he returned after his shower, Omar said, "Tess, can you please get up? It's time to brush your teeth and take a shower."

She got up and walked to her bathroom, Jack following behind. "I put a fresh towel and some new clothes over there for you," he said, pointing while avoiding eye contact. "There's a scrunchie on top if you don't want to get your hair wet." He turned the shower on. "I'll be right outside the door, sweetheart. You can let me know when you're done."

He walked away and stood outside the bathroom door, which he left slightly ajar.

When Tess finished, she opened the door and stood behind him. He was about to move out of her way, but she reached out and touched his hand. He inhaled deeply, and in a gentle voice said, "I love you with my whole heart, forever. I'm here when you're ready."

She stood for a moment before moving her hand. He stepped aside and she walked past him. In the kitchen, Omar pulled out a barstool for her. "I made you some oatmeal and there's a glass of orange juice. Please sit and try to eat a little something."

Jack caught Omar's eye. "Something happened." Before he could continue, he noticed Tess putting her hand on her neck. "Her necklace, she's looking for it," he said, as he darted off.

He returned a moment later and handed the necklace to Omar. "Tess, is this what you're looking for?" Omar asked, placing it in front of her. "It was a gift from Jack. It's very special to you."

She picked it up, clutched it tightly, and squeezed her eyelids shut. She opened her eyes and in a quiet voice, she said, "Jack's heart. His whole heart. Forever." She looked up. "Omar, where's Jack?"

"I'm right here, baby," Jack said, diving in front of her. "I'm right here."

She burst into tears. "Jack, I need you."

He threw his arms around her and pressed her tightly against him. "I'm right here. It's okay. I'm here. I've got you."

She couldn't stop wailing. Jack scooped her up in his arms and carried her to the couch. She didn't let go of him. He pressed his forehead to hers, stroked her hair, and quietly said, "It's okay, I'm here. I'm here."

"I'm not safe," she cried.

"Why aren't you safe?" he asked, holding her firmly.

She pulled back to look at him. He rubbed her shoulder with one hand and her face with the other. "Because he found me," she sobbed.

"Who found you?"

"I can't tell you."

"Why can't you tell me?"

Her cries were only getting louder; her whole body was shaking. Through her gasps, she said, "Because I'm afraid he'll take me away. I want to stay here with you. I just want to be with you. Please don't let anyone separate us. I'm not Essie. I'm not Essie. I'm Tess Miller. Please, Jack."

"No one is taking you anywhere. No one is going to separate us. I won't allow it. I promise. You can tell me. Who found you?"

"My father. My father found me," she said before collapsing onto his chest.

"It's okay, baby. Everything is going to be okay. You're safe. I won't let anyone hurt you ever again. I've got you."

Ten minutes later, still curled tightly into a ball on Jack's lap, Tess muttered, "I'm so tired."

"I know, sweetheart. Let's go lie down."

"Okay," she said.

"I'm just going to talk to Omar for a minute."

"Please come right back."

Omar placed the orange juice and oatmeal in front of her. "Butterfly, it would be good if you took a few bites."

"I'm not hungry," she whimpered.

"Maybe you can try. At least have a little of your juice," Omar said.

Jack stood slowly, still holding her hand. Tess looked up at him with fearful eyes. "I promise, I'll be right back," he assured her.

Jack and Omar walked into the kitchen but remained where Tess could see them. In a hushed voice, Jack asked, "What do you know about her father?"

Omar shook his head. "Nothing. She told me her grandfather and uncle abused her. She never said a word about anyone else, only that she wanted nothing to do with anyone from her family."

"We need to find out exactly where he is. Call Bobby and ask him to locate him and to call when he has information. I'm not going to leave Tess, so tell him to call you or leave me a voicemail."

"Okay," Omar said. "Jack, we need to know what he did to her and why she's so afraid. It's the only way to help her. After she gets some rest, I think we should try to get a proper meal into her, watch one of her favorite movies or something to relax, and if she seems like she can handle it, we need to ask her. Since you're the one she's opening up to, I think you should do it. I'll stay in your sight line and let you know if I think you should stop. She's in a fragile state and we don't want to cause any more trauma."

"All right," Jack said.

"She might reveal that he also raped her, so we need to be prepared to hear whatever she tells us."

"Yeah, I know."

Omar put his hand on Jack's shoulder. "Now I understand why she told Vivian her name is Mrs. Miller. It's her identity. She doesn't fear what someone will do to her, but that she will be separated from you. It's important you assure her that's never going to happen. She needs to feel safe and connected. Whatever you can do to make her feel that way, you should do."

"I understand."

"And she shouldn't be alone. We don't have a complete picture of her state of mind yet. We should err on the side of caution."

"Okay, I understand," Jack said.

"You haven't said much. Are you okay, Jack?"

"I am, now that Tess has come back to us. I'm just eager to be with her, to help her, to stop feeling so damn useless."

They walked back into the living room. "I drank some juice," Tess said.

Jack smiled. "Let's go get some rest, sweetheart." He took her hand and led her into their bedroom.

"I need to go to the bathroom," she said.

"I'll wait right here," he said, standing near the door.

When she came out he took her hand and they walked over to their bed. She climbed in and lay on her side, facing him. He crawled in beside her and put his hand on her shoulder.

"How are you doing?" he asked.

"I don't know." She started to tear up.

"It's okay," he said, tucking her hair behind her ear.

"It's so lonely without you. I missed you," she said.

"I missed you, too. More than you could know." He leaned forward and lightly pressed his lips to hers.

"I missed that," she whispered.

"Me too." He kissed her again. "I love you more than anything."

"I love you, too," she said. "Jack, I'm so tired."

"I know. Let's get some sleep."

"Promise you won't leave."

"I promise. I'm not going anywhere."

She turned around and he wrapped his arms around her. They closed their eyes and were soon fast asleep.

***

Five hours later, they awoke in exactly the same position in which they fell asleep. Tess ran her fingers against Jack's hand.

"Hey," he whispered.

"I'm going to freshen up," she said. She got up and went to the bathroom. A few minutes later, she emerged with a clean face.

"My turn," Jack said, grazing her arm as he walked past her.

When he returned, Tess was curled up in the chair in the corner of the room, crying.

He rushed over, knelt before her, and took her hand. "It's okay. I'm here."

"Jack, I'm so sorry."

"You have nothing to be sorry for."

"I'm not strong like you," she sniveled.

"Tess, you're the strongest person I know. For most of my life, I had to block out all my feelings, stop seeing people. You've experienced the worst of what people can do and you still look everyone in the eye and see their humanity. You choose love, always. I couldn't do that. I'm in awe of you, Tess Miller. I will never be as strong as you are."

She ran her fingers through his hair.

"Gracie punctured my heart and then you cracked it wide open. Before the two of you, I had stopped myself from feeling."

"But I'm such a terrible burden."

"That isn't true. Please don't think that for a minute."

"I can see it on your face. You're so worried and it's my fault."

"Sweetheart, of course I'm worried. I hate to see you hurting. But that doesn't mean you're a burden. I'm honored to take care of you. People who love each other take care of each other; you take care of me all the time. You're the kindest, most wonderful person I've ever known."

She shook her head. "That isn't true. I'm selfish."

"Why are you saying that?" he asked.

"Because you want to save the world, and I just want you to save me."

"Oh sweetheart, come here." He pulled her close and she put her arms around him. "We'll get through this. I promise. Besides, this is what

I signed up to do. I will protect you from the darkness, with my whole heart, forever. For now, I think we should go eat something. You'll feel better with some food in you. Come on," he said, helping her rise.

She grabbed a tissue from the nightstand to clean herself up, took his hand, and followed him into the kitchen.

"Well good afternoon, sleepy heads," Omar said. "Are you feeling more rested?"

"Uh huh," Tess muttered.

"Something smells good in here," Jack said.

"I had Thai food delivered, all of Tess's favorites. Dishes and chopsticks are already set out in the living room. Jack, can you help me with the food and drinks?"

"Why don't you go sit down," Jack said to Tess. "We'll be right there."

Tess shuffled into the living room and collapsed onto the sofa.

"How's she doing?" Omar asked quietly.

"She slept, but then when I came out of the bathroom she was crying. She told me she's not strong and she feels like a burden. It wasn't good. I don't know if I said the right things or got through to her."

"Tess has always cared more about other people than herself, so I was concerned that's where her mind would go. We'll just have to keep reinforcing the message. The very last thing we want her thinking is that she's a burden."

"Any word from Bobby?" Jack asked.

"He located her father. He lives in a retirement home in Rhode Island and was admitted to a local hospital three days ago. Bobby's having trouble getting more information. He hasn't been able to confirm if he's still there. He said he'd find out and get back to us as soon as possible."

"Okay."

"The best thing we can do right now is try to get some food in her and ease her into a better frame of mind. If you'll grab the drinks, I'll bring the food in."

Jack nodded.

Omar set the containers on the coffee table. "We've got loads of pad Thai, steamed veggies, summer rolls, and peanut sauce. All your favorites, Tess. And here's chicken and rice for Jack."

"Thank you," Jack said, placing sparkling waters in front of each of them and taking a seat on the couch beside Tess.

"I figured you both must be starving," Omar said.

"Yeah," Jack said.

"All of a sudden, I feel famished. It all smells good," Tess said. "Thank you."

"My pleasure." Omar replied. "Well, I thought we could use some fun so we're going to watch one of your favorite movies. *Cinema Paradiso* has subtitles, so that's out. You only watch *Breakfast at Tiffany's* when you're in New York, so that won't work. That leaves us with my personal favorite, our old standby, *Moulin Rouge*, which is all set and ready to go."

"Oh, I don't think Jack will like that."

"Nonsense," Omar rebuffed.

Tess turned to Jack. "It's a love story and a musical."

"And it's Tess's favorite film," Omar said.

"If you love it, I'm sure I will too," Jack said.

Tess shrugged. "Okay."

"You have to tell me once and for all what you love most about this movie. Is it the spectacular sets?" Omar asked.

"They are wonderful, but no."

"The big musical numbers?"

"Also wonderful, but no."

"Then it must be the message, that to love and be loved is the greatest gift of all."

"I do love that, but no. I'm not telling."

"Butterfly, did you ever tell Jack about that time in Chicago?" Omar asked, plopping down in a recliner.

"I had been on the road for what seemed like ages doing book events. I hadn't seen Omar in months because he was busy with grad school, which was torture, so we were going to meet in Chicago. Of course, somewhere in Illinois I got a nasty cold. By the time I got to Chicago, I was deathly sick."

"And let me tell you Jack, she's an absolute monster when she's sick."

"I can't believe that," Jack said.

"Oh, it's true. First, there's the nightmare of getting her to admit that she's sick. Then there's taking care of her. She gets very grumpy. It's brutal."

Tess giggled. "It's true. I hate being sick."

"The only good thing that happens when you get sick is that it reminds me you're human. You're so impossibly wonderful all the time, that sometimes I wonder. Then you get a cold and turn into a little beast. It's quite reassuring."

Tess smiled. "Being the marvelous friend that he is, Omar stayed with me in my hotel suite since I wasn't up to going out. We ordered loads of room service, all junk, like baskets of French fries, and we watched *Moulin Rouge* for like the fifth time."

"Nice try, it was more like the twenty-fifth time," Omar protested.

"Wait, you ate French fries?" Jack asked Tess.

She nodded. "A whole basket of them. I was so loopy from the cold medicine I didn't know what I was doing, or maybe I didn't care. Omar wanted to cheer me up, so he acted out every single musical number in the entire movie. I mean, dancing and belting out every song. I had been so grouchy but I couldn't help but laugh and smile. It was splendid. Thank goodness he has a gorgeous voice."

"And then of course there's 'Your Song,' which you and I always do together. Even sick as a dog, I made you get out of bed for that one."

Tess laughed. "I remember." She paused and looked a bit melancholy. "We had some fun times."

"And we'll have many more, Butterfly."

"I hope so," Tess replied.

"I think it's time to hit play," Omar said, grabbing the remote. "Take some food, guys."

Tess helped herself to a modest portion of pad Thai and steamed vegetables. She ate slowly while the movie played. When her dish was empty, she took more pad Thai and a summer roll. Omar smiled inconspicuously at Jack.

Right before "Your Song" came on, Omar said, "You know what's coming."

"Oh, I don't think I'm up to it," Tess said.

"Well I am. You're not going to leave me on my own, are you?"

The song began and Omar leapt up, took Tess's hand, and began singing to her. When he belted out the words "if they're green or they're blue," she stood up, smiling. They started dancing across the room, in perfect unison with the film. At one point, Omar jumped onto a chair and opened an umbrella he had stashed away. Tess laughed. Jack watched, grinning from ear to ear, relief and love washing over him. At the end, Omar twirled Tess out and back to him, spun her up in his arms, and then the grand dip. When she stood upright, they were both smiling and laughing. Jack clapped.

"We've never done that for an audience before," Tess said. She sat down and looked at Omar. "What would I do without you?"

"You'll never have to find out," he replied.

Tess nestled into Jack and they watched the rest of the movie. When it was over, she looked up at him expectantly. "Well, what did you think?"

"It was great. But I have to say, my favorite part was your dance with Omar. You two have such a beautiful friendship."

"Yeah, I got pretty lucky with men later in life," Tess said.

"How about some tea, guys?" Omar asked.

"Sure," Tess said.

"I'll put the leftovers away and make a pot," he replied.

"I'll help you," Jack said.

"I've got it. You stay with Tess," Omar replied.

Tess and Jack cuddled on the couch. "How are you doing?" he asked.

"Better."

He kissed the top of her head.

Soon, Omar returned with a tray carrying a teapot and cups. "It's chamomile. That's soothing," he said, pouring it into the teacups.

Tess sat up. "Thank you."

Omar took his seat and nodded at Jack.

"Sweetheart, we wanted to talk to you."

"What's wrong?" she asked, turning to him.

"Nothing's wrong. We don't want to upset you, so if you're not up to it, it's perfectly okay," he said, rubbing her back. "We just wanted to ask you a couple of questions. About your father, Tess. It would help me protect you if I knew a little more."

"Okay," she said softly.

"What did he say when he called?"

"He just said, 'Hello Essie.' I said, 'I don't want to talk to you.' Then he said, 'If you don't talk to me, I'm going to call your husband.' I got scared and hung up. Then, I smashed my phone so he couldn't call back. I'm sorry; I guess my phone is ruined."

"That's okay. We can get you a new one," Jack said. He glanced up at Omar, who gestured for him to continue. He took her hands. "I would never ask you anything to hurt you; I only want to help you. You know that, right?"

"Yes."

"Sweetheart, when you were growing up, did your father hurt you, like those other men?"

"No. Never."

Relief started to sweep across Jack's face, but then Tess continued. "What he did was much worse. It's the worst thing anyone has ever done to me."

Jack held Tess's face in both of his hands. He swallowed and said, "You can tell me."

"I couldn't take it anymore. So, I summoned all the strength I had and I went to my father to tell him what was happening. I told him what they did to me. Jack, I told him everything I could manage to say out loud." Her eyes began to tear but she continued, speaking very slowly as if she was reliving it. "I told him how they would bring me to the basement, lock the door, make me take off my clothes, and cover my head, and then I told him the terrible things they did to me. I told him how I begged them to stop." Jack saw Omar stand up, sobbing so hard he had to turn away. Jack's eyes flooded, but he held her face, looking straight into her eyes. "I told him, and he said, 'Okay.' I thought that meant it was over, that he would do something. But he didn't do anything. He let them do whatever they wanted. They were welcome in that house any time. Maybe he didn't believe me or maybe he just didn't care. What he did to me was that he did *nothing*. *Nothing* to save me from the darkness."

Jack pulled her to his chest, his arms huddled around her head. "I'm so sorry. I'm so sorry," he said through his tears.

"Nothing changed after that day, except they didn't lock the door anymore," she whimpered.

"I'm so sorry, Tess. You're safe now. I promise."

"Did I help?" she asked.

"Yeah, baby. You helped."

He held Tess for a long time, until her breathing had slowed to normal and her body relaxed. After comforting Tess, Jack leaned back, looked into her eyes, and gently asked, "Are you okay?"

"Yeah."

"Why don't you drink your tea and try to relax. Do you want me to put the TV on?"

"Okay," she said.

He put it on and handed her the remote. "Find something light to watch. I'll be right back."

She took the remote and started flipping through stations. Jack walked into the kitchen and found Omar on the floor in the far corner of the room. He was having trouble catching his breath. Jack rushed over, knelt down, and put his hands on Omar's shoulders. "Try to slow your breath. Try to slow your breath. Deep breaths, in… and out. Focus on your breathing. That's it," he said, as Omar's breathing steadied.

"They covered her head, Jack. They covered her head," Omar gasped.

"I know."

"That's why she can't walk past a stranger without looking them in the eyes. How could anyone do that to her?"

Jack shook his head.

"I'm sorry," Omar said, wiping his eyes. "It's just so painful to imagine anyone hurting her like that. The damage they've done."

"I know."

"I'm all right now," Omar said, rising. "We should sit with Tess."

"Why don't you go splash some water on your face? Take a minute for yourself. I'm going to call Bobby, but I'll stay nearby."

Omar nodded and walked off.

Jack dialed Bobby's number. When Bobby answered, Jack quietly said, "Did you find her father? I just found out what he did to her."

"He's dead, Jack. He died early this morning. Cancer. That's why I had trouble getting info from the hospital – they were waiting to inform his next of kin."

"Okay, thanks," Jack said. "I'll talk to you tomorrow."

Jack waited for Omar to return. "Her father's dead. It happened early this morning."

"He must have wanted to speak to her before he died," Omar surmised.

"Yeah," Jack said. "Maybe Tess will feel better if we tell her. She won't have to be afraid anymore."

"We do need to tell her, but there's no way to know how she will feel. It's always complex with family, which is why this kind of abuse is so horrific. I don't know what her response will be."

They joined Tess in the living room. Jack sat beside her on the couch. She put her tea down and looked at him. He smiled. "What is it?" she asked.

Omar grabbed the remote control and turned off the TV.

"Sweetheart, your father died," Jack said.

A look of confusion swept across her face. "Did…"

"He died early this morning. He had cancer."

She sat silently for a moment before saying, "So, he knew he was dying when he called?"

"Yes," Jack replied.

"Do you think he was calling to apologize?" she asked.

"I don't know."

"I'm glad I hung up. Now I can always imagine he was calling to say he was sorry."

CHAPTER 11

The next morning, Jack and Tess lay in bed, snuggling.

"How are you feeling, sweetheart?" Jack asked.

"Like I just want to stay like this for as long as possible, with you."

"There's nowhere else we need to be," he replied.

An hour later, they rolled out of bed. Omar was in the kitchen reading the newspaper, containers of berries and a basket of fruit on the bar. He put the paper down. "Well, good morning. Butterfly, you've given me a complex about my cooking, so I went out and bought you some fruit for breakfast."

She kissed the top of his head. "Thank you."

"I'll make a fresh pot of coffee," Jack said.

"Then after breakfast, perhaps we can go out and get some fresh air. It would be good for you, Butterfly," Omar said.

"Okay," Tess agreed.

Omar smiled. "I was hoping you would say that. I took the liberty of calling Denise and making you an appointment for your blowout, since you missed your usual time."

"Is that your way of saying I'm having a bad hair day?" she asked.

"Well, I don't want kick you while you're down, but it's dreadful. I mean really, Butterfly, we have standards to adhere to."

Tess giggled, picked a grape out of the basket, and flung it at his head.

Jack grinned.

"I thought I could keep you company at the salon and Jack could go down the block to get you a new cell phone."

"How does that sound, sweetheart?" Jack asked.

"Fine," Tess said, biting into a strawberry.

***

Later, Jack and Omar escorted Tess to the hair salon. They barely had time to sit down in the waiting area when Denise came bounding out to greet Tess. She pulled her away so quickly that Jack and Omar couldn't say a word. Omar turned to Jack, "You should go get her phone so you'll be back here when she's done. I called ahead, and it should be ready to pick up."

Jack's face looked pained.

"She'll be fine," Omar said. "I'm right here and you'll only be a couple of blocks away."

Jack reluctantly nodded and left. Forty-five minutes later, he returned with a phone and a whole bag of accessories. "How's she doing?" he asked, taking the seat beside Omar.

"She's been blabbing on and on with Denise like they always do. This was the perfect way to start to reintegrate her into normal life. She'll be done any minute."

Tess appeared from the back of the salon. "So, what do you think? Am I suitable for viewing?"

"Gorgeous, Butterfly," Omar said. "Much better than that bird's nest you were sporting."

She laughed and hit his arm. "You're terrible."

"And what do you think, Mr. Miller?" she asked.

"I think you're perfect, Mrs. Miller," he said.

***

When they got back to the house, Omar said, "What do you feel like doing, Butterfly? You haven't written in days. Maybe you want to try. Or if you're not up to it, we could torture Jack with some more of our favorite movies."

"You are the absolute sweetest and I couldn't survive without you, but I think you should go home," she replied.

"I'm happy to stay here as long as you like," he replied.

"I know and I love you for it, but you have a handsome man of your own waiting at home. He probably thinks you defected by now!" she joked.

Jack and Omar looked at her with serious expressions.

"It's okay. I'm with Jack. I feel lighter than I have in days – in years, really," she said.

"You know I'm just a phone call away," Omar said, walking over and taking her hand. "I can be here in a heartbeat."

She hugged him. "I know. I love you more than words."

"Sweetheart, do you mind if I speak with Omar for a minute?" Jack asked.

She smiled. "Of course not. I'm going to go get comfy and change into sweats."

Tess left the room and Jack turned to Omar. "I'm just worried about her. She seems a lot better today, but..."

"I know," Omar replied. "It's going to take time. She's been through an intense trauma and she's still processing it. Just be with her. She feels safe with you. It would be good for Tess to start working again, too. Writing has always been her truest friend. I don't think she should be alone for at least a few more days, maybe longer."

"We can hang out here for the rest of the weekend and then I'll just call out of work again next week," Jack said.

"That's one option, but I'm not sure it's the best plan. She needs normalcy, and part of that is you returning to work. Is it possible for her to go to work with you? Do you have a desk or office or somewhere you can put her? That way she'd have to get up in the morning and start working, and she'd have some independence, but you could keep an eye on her."

"Yes, there's a conference room two doors down from my office. She could come all week, or longer. She can see Joe and Bobby, too. I can keep everyone else out of there."

"That sounds perfect. Bring it up when the time is right and see what she thinks," Omar said.

Jack nodded. "Omar, I don't know how to thank you for everything."

"There's no need. Tess is my family, and now you are too. I would do anything for her. Please, don't hesitate for a minute to call. I can be back here any time."

"Thank you," Jack said.

***

Jack and Tess spent the rest of the afternoon watching TV and eating leftover Thai food. The next morning, they exercised together before breakfast. Tess took a mug of coffee and said she was going up to her office. Jack followed behind with the Sunday newspaper. When he walked into the office, Tess was standing at her desk, brushing her fingertips across the top of her laptop. He kissed her on the cheek. "Why don't you try writing?" he suggested.

"Oh, I don't know," she mumbled.

"Well, you can try if you want to. I have this to get through," he said, holding up the large newspaper. "I'll sit over there in the corner. If you get bored, you can come hang out with me."

He sat down and opened the newspaper. Tess sat at her desk, staring at him. Finally, she put on her reading glasses, opened her laptop, and began working. Two hours later, she turned off her computer, strolled over to Jack, and plopped onto his lap. "How's it going, baby?" he asked.

"It's going. But I'm done for today. Let's go watch a movie or something. I'll miss you so much tomorrow when you go back to work."

"Actually, I was hoping you'd come with me. There's an empty office you can use and that way we can see each other all day."

She smiled. "I like the sound of that."

"Good," he said, kissing her.

CHAPTER 12

On Monday morning, they both got ready to go to Jack's office for the day. Jack asked Joe to go in early and tell everyone the conference room was off-limits for the week. Tess was in the kitchen, filling two tumblers with coffee when Jack walked in.

He kissed the top of her head. "You look nice. Almost ready?"

"I'm ready now," she said, handing him his coffee.

"We have some time if you want to have breakfast," he said.

"I'm not hungry. Let's go," she replied, grabbing her work bag.

***

They walked into the office and were immediately greeted by Joe.

"Great to see you, Tess," he said, giving her a peck on the cheek.

"You too," she replied.

"I'm going to get Tess situated," Jack said.

Jack led Tess into the oval-shaped conference room, with glass windows all around overlooking cubicles and other offices. He set up her laptop at the table. "There's coffee and tea over there," he said, pointing to the corner. "You know where my office is, just over there," he said, motioning.

"Thanks. I'll be fine," she said.

"I'll stop in to check on you, but you can come get me anytime you need me."

"Okay."

"Bobby, Joe, and I will have lunch with you later. Bobby's going to pick something up. What do you want?"

"Oh, uh, just some fruit is fine."

There was a knock on the door and Bobby came vaulting in. "Hey, you," he said to Tess with a huge hug. "So glad you're feeling better."

"Thank you for everything."

"Nah, that's what friends are for. Well, I don't want to intrude. I just wanted to say hi and welcome. I'll stop in again later and you can always find me if you want to," he said, leaving the room.

"Hey, come here," Jack said when they were alone, pulling her near. He embraced her tightly and kissed her. "I guess I should get to work if you don't need anything."

"I'm fine, really," she said.

He left the room but stopped outside the door to peer in. Tess had already put on her reading glasses and begun typing. He took a deep breath and went to his office. Joe was waiting for him.

"Tess looks good," Joe said. "You're a different story. You look like you've been through the ringer."

"I'm just worried about her. I don't like leaving her alone."

"It's good for her to work. She knows how to find you. Try not to worry. Bobby and I will check in on her, too. She's safe here."

"Thanks," Jack mumbled.

***

Between Jack, Joe, and Bobby, someone stopped in to check on Tess every half hour. At noon, they came bounding into the room with lunch. Bobby placed two white paper bags on the table.

"I must have lost track of time," Tess said, taking off her glasses and closing her laptop.

Joe smiled at Jack.

"Hi, sweetheart," Jack said, kissing the top of her head and taking the seat beside her. "How's your day going?"

"It's going. What about you?"

"Pretty uneventful around here, which is always a good thing," he replied.

Bobby started doling out the food. He placed a colorful fruit salad in front of Tess and slid sandwiches to Jack and Joe. Then he took out two extra sandwiches. He unwrapped one of them. "Jack said you eat grilled cheese with pickles in it, which is super weird. I like weird, so I decided to try it. It's my second sandwich, so I'm only going to eat half of it. You're welcome to have the other half," he said, placing it between them.

"Thanks," she said, picking up her half and biting into it.

Bobby took a mouthful. "Wow, this is actually really good. I'd never have thought of it. So, what are you working on, Tess?"

"Years ago, I wrote a collection of essays about the power of literature. My publisher has been trying to get me to release a new edition for ages, and I finally agreed. It's perfect timing, actually. I could use a little break from fiction, which is so much more draining."

They spent the next half hour talking and eating. Joe and Bobby picked up the garbage while Jack had a moment with Tess.

"You doing okay?" he asked, stroking her arm.

"Yeah. Baby, you don't have to worry so much."

"You know where to find me if you need me. I love you."

"I love you, too."

Tess opened her laptop and put her glasses back on. The guys left the room. As soon as the door was shut, Jack said, "Holy shit, Bobby, you're like the food whisperer."

Bobby laughed. "Glad to help."

"She really seems like she's doing as well as she could be, under the circumstances," Joe said.

"Yeah," Jack said, visibly more relaxed.

***

Tess continued working for the next two and a half hours, and Jack, Bobby, and Joe continued to pop in to say hello. Just after three o'clock, Chris walked into the conference room, ostensibly to get a cup of coffee.

"Hi, Tess," he said.

"Hello," she replied, busy on her keyboard.

"I guess I didn't get the memo that it's bring-your-wife-to-work day. I suppose when you're the boss, you think you can do whatever you want, huh?"

"What?" Tess asked.

"Oh, nothing. I mean, Jack's the man. If he wants you here, that's his call. I just don't think it looks very good for him. See ya!"

He took his coffee and left.

Tess noticed Bobby walking by and she jumped up and swung the door open.

"Hey, Tess. Are you okay?" Bobby asked.

"Is it bad for Jack that I'm here? Please, you have to tell me the truth."

"No, not at all. What are you talking about?"

"Chris just came into the conference room and told me that it wasn't good for Jack that I'm here. The last thing I want is to cause trouble for him or to be a burden. Should I leave?"

"Absolutely not. Please, just sit tight. I'll be right back."

Bobby made a beeline to Jack's office, where Jack and Joe were reviewing a document. "Jack, please stay calm, but something happened."

Jack jumped up.

"Apparently, Chris went into the conference room and said something to Tess about how her being here is causing a problem for you."

"He did *what*?" Jack bellowed.

"She asked me if it was a burden for you that she's here."

A look of rage washed across his face. He opened his top desk drawer, pulled out a gun, and sprinted out of the room before anyone could stop him.

Bobby and Joe followed, hollering, "Jack, you need to calm down."

Tess watched as he flew by the conference room.

Jack dragged Chris out of his chair and slammed him against the wall, jamming an arm under his neck. "What the fuck did you say to my wife?" he screamed.

Chris was too stunned to reply.

"Jack, calm down. Think about what you're doing," Joe said.

"What the fuck did you say to her?" Jack screeched.

Tess heard the commotion and came running over just as Jack jammed his gun into Chris's temple. "I'll fucking kill you. Nobody hurts her," he screamed.

Tess was trembling. "Jack, please, put the gun down. I'm not hurt."

"You're scaring Tess," Bobby said. "Put the gun down."

Tess walked up to Jack, placed her hand on his shoulder, and softly said, "Please, Jack. Put the gun down. Please, baby."

Jack was still shaking but he lowered the gun and stepped back. He handed the weapon to Bobby and let Chris go. He turned to Tess, but couldn't look her in the eyes. "I'm sorry. I'm sorry."

"It's okay," she said. "Let's walk away."

"I'll take you back to the conference room," he mumbled. Tess wrapped an arm around him and led him back to the conference room. "I'm sorry," he said. "Please stay here. I just need a minute."

He went to his office where Bobby was waiting for him. He shut the door, hunched over, and broke down into tears. "I can't believe I did that. What's wrong with me? She already thinks it's bad for me to have her here and now I've proved it to her because I can't fucking control myself." He covered his face with his hands. "I've made everything worse."

Joe let himself in and closed the door behind him. "Listen, I told Chris what's going on."

"You know how private she is. Why did you do that?" Jack asked, still hysterical.

"I didn't tell him the details, just that Tess was the victim of a crime and that she's here so you can keep an eye on her. He felt terrible. He's not going to file a report. No one who saw what happened is going to say anything."

Jack tried to regain his composure, but his face was bright red and his breathing was out of control. "I don't know what to say to Tess to fix this."

"Let me talk to her," Joe offered.

"I don't know," Jack replied, pacing.

"Listen, I didn't tell either of you this, but I had a health scare a few months ago. They thought it might be cancer. I needed to bring someone with me to the oncologist, so I asked Tess."

"She never told me that," Jack said.

"I asked her to keep it private. It turned out to be a false alarm, but we spent hours waiting and talking. She told me how traumatic her childhood was and that being with you is the first time she's felt safe or happy. I confessed to her that I am lonely and that watching you two together makes me wish I had someone to share my life with. I asked her what it is that makes your bond so strong, and without missing a beat, she said, 'Like a puzzle, our broken pieces fit together.'"

Joe's words seemed to comfort Jack, who was slowly pulling himself together.

"She knows you're not perfect, Jack. Please, let me go talk to her. I think I can help."

Jack nodded.

Joe knocked on the door to the conference room before opening it. Tess was walking in circles. "Is Jack okay?" she asked.

"He feels very badly for upsetting you and he's ashamed of himself, but he'll be okay. May I speak with you for a minute?"

"Of course."

"Please, let's sit down," he said. "Jack is feeling especially protective of you right now because you've gone through something so painful. It's natural that he would feel that way. He loves you, Tess. Chris is a massive jerk; you know he's been riding Jack for a long time. It has nothing to do with you. Emotions are high, so things got a little out of hand, but the last thing Jack wants is for you to think that you're causing a problem for him. Nothing could be further from the truth. The best thing you can do for him is to try to move past what happened here. Will you please stay?"

"Okay," she said.

Joe smiled. "Thank you, Tess. I'll let you get back to your work."

She grabbed his arm. "Please keep an eye on him for me."

"I will."

Joe smiled and left the room. After he shut the door, he saw Tess put on her glasses and open her laptop. He went back to Jack's office.

"She's fine," he said.

"Are you sure?" Jack asked.

"Yes. She's working. You can go see for yourself. She asked me to keep an eye on you. She's worried about you."

"Thank you," Jack said, and he went to go check on Tess. He stood in the hall and watched her typing. He took a deep breath and walked away before she could see him.

***

For the rest of the day, Tess kept working and Bobby and Joe stopped by occasionally to check on her, but Jack stayed holed up in his office and kept his distance. Tired of waiting for him, Tess got up to stretch her legs and found herself in Jack's office. "Hey, stranger. How are you holding up?"

"Hey," he said, coming around his desk to greet her. "I'm so sorry, sweetheart."

"You don't have to be sorry," she said, reaching out for his hand. "I just want to know you're all right."

"I feel awful for upsetting you. I completely lost it."

"Chris is an ass," Tess said.

He laughed.

"But Jack, that's not really what's going on here. This wasn't about Chris. You want to save me from things that happened decades ago, from the people who hurt me. But you can't."

He looked down, unable to meet her gaze.

"Jack, you can't. What's in the past can't be changed. Knowing vaguely about it is one thing, but hearing all the details may have been too much, and ..."

"Hey," he interrupted, rubbing her arm, "I wanted you to tell me. You can always tell me anything."

"It was still a lot to process. I want you to know that I understand why you're feeling so protective. Don't you think I feel something every day when I see the scars on your body? Don't you think I would give anything to take that pain away? But I know that I can't, so instead, they remind me to show you every single day how much I love you, and to always be gentle with you. Can you please try to do the same thing? You can't save me from the past, but you can be with me now. That's all I want."

He brushed his fingers across her cheek. "Yes, I can do that."

"Let's go home."

CHAPTER 13

The next morning, Tess showered and got ready for the day. "Your turn, honey," she said. He grazed her hand as he passed by. Twenty minutes later, he came into the kitchen and found Tess sticking an empty oatmeal bowl in the sink. He smiled discretely. "Here," she said, handing him a coffee tumbler, and they headed to his office.

***

Jack, Joe, and Bobby checked on Tess less frequently than they had the previous day. Everyone was settling into a comfortable routine. At noon, they came into the conference room with a huge platter of sushi. Bobby distributed chopsticks, paper plates, and bottled water. Tess was leaning against the wall, talking on her cell phone.

"Hang on a minute," she said to the person on the phone. She turned to Jack. "Hi, baby."

He kissed her. "What's going on?"

"There's going to be a bidding war for the Chinese translation rights to my new book."

"That's great, sweetheart."

She smiled. "I just need a couple of minutes to finish this call, fellas. Please eat, I'll be right there."

"We'll wait," Bobby said as he and Joe sat down.

Tess shifted her focus back to her phone call. "Hey, Crystal. Please read his message." She listened for a moment and then said, "Wow, respect and loyalty? That almost made me laugh out loud. Let me think." She closed her eyes in thought and then said, "Okay, here's my response. Are you ready? Dear Tihao, Thank you for your interest in expanding our relationship. I'm sure you know that the only reason we are having this conversation is because I operate from a place of respect and loyalty. That does not mean, however, that I have replaced my backbone with a wishbone. The terms we offered are fair and non-negotiable. We both know that if I allow this to go to an open bidding war, the price will be much higher. I trust we are clear on what the deal is. I don't want any last-minute changes. Beyond the royalty structure, there is a non-recoupable licensing fee. Do not attempt to roll it into an advance. If you're going to use words like respect and loyalty, you should honor them. Please stop dragging your feet. You have seventy-two hours to send a signed contract. Otherwise, we'll go to an open bid and I'll spend my next holiday in Beijing or Shanghai instead of Taipei. I look forward to hearing from you directly, not from your lawyers." Tess paused. "Crystal, did you get all that? Okay, add a paragraph at the end that reads: I hope your mother is doing well. You are all in my thoughts. Tess." She paused and said, "Yup, that's it. Please send it immediately. Gotta go. Bye."

Tess hung up and Jack pulled out a chair for her to take a seat. Bobby and Joe stared with their mouths agape.

"Sorry about that," she said.

"That was awesome," Bobby said.

"What?" Tess asked.

"It's just that you're literally the nicest person we know, but you're such a badass. I mean, 'I haven't replaced my backbone with a wishbone' and the 'respect and loyalty' stuff. Savage. Priceless."

Tess laughed.

"I'm in awe," Joe said. "Truly, you're the most impressive person I've ever met, Tess."

She blushed. "You're overly kind."

"Not at all. I sincerely mean it. I've thought it since the day I met you," Joe replied.

Jack rubbed Tess's back. "I know. I'm more amazed by her every day."

"And then you asked about his mother and sounded so genuine," Bobby said. "How do you do that when someone's jerking you around?"

"His mother has Alzheimer's. It's very difficult for him. He is simultaneously someone with whom I'm having a professional wrestling match, and also, a human being who is dealing with a difficult personal situation. I can hold two thoughts." She cracked open her water bottle and took a sip.

"I can't stare at this sushi anymore without eating it. Let's eat," Joe said, gesturing toward the platter. "Tess, the veggie rolls are in front of you."

"Thank you," she said, as they all helped themselves.

"Why not let it go to a bidding war and drive up the price?" Bobby asked.

"I know which publisher I want to work with for reasons that are more important to me than financial terms. For example, we'll have an easier time slipping past the censors with a Taiwanese publisher. If I allow it to go to an open bid, there's tremendous pressure to take the highest offer. If I don't, it puts me in a terrible spot for future negotiations. I'm trying to make this happen beforehand, so I can control the outcome."

"Tess, I've always been curious about your approach to negotiations. I've heard that the two most important things are the ability to walk away and being armed with information. Do you agree?" Joe asked.

"That's the common wisdom, but no, I don't agree. It's better if you're able to walk away, but that isn't always the case. Sometimes we have to play ball with people whether we like it or not. I'm sure you encounter that in your work all the time. And having as much information as you can is certainly a good thing, but the facts aren't always on your side. Most people rely on those two things to win negotiations, but they will betray you because you can't control them. You should walk into every negotiation with something you can control. There's a third factor that I think is most important at the end of the day, and that's the story, the vision you are selling. The more you believe it, the better you can persuade others, even when the facts don't support you."

"Brilliant," Joe said.

"That's my Tess," Jack said, staring lovingly at her.

"It's not just business, either. Do you remember the story my friend Abdul told you at our wedding about passing through that mob?"

They nodded.

"My goal in that situation was to make sure he was safe. The facts were certainly not on our side, nor were we able to walk away and avoid it. Despite the advice from the security team, it was clear to me that the situation was going to get worse and we needed to move as quickly as possible. But first, I needed to make Abdul believe we could do it. So, we chanted until I could see that he believed. That's how we made it through that day. Of course, something terrible could have happened to us anyway, but without him believing it was possible to get to the other side in one piece, we wouldn't have had a chance."

"Did you believe?" Jack asked softly.

She looked at him.

"That there's only darkness and light and that love is the bridge between them?"

"Yes, with all my heart," she said.

Jack smiled. "Thank God you made it."

"So Tess, do you think you'll get that Chinese contract you want?" Bobby asked.

"Yes, within twenty-four hours, and I'll hear from Tihao before that, likely trying to smooth things over. It's a little after noon here, which means it's midnight in Taipei. Tihao suffers from insomnia and often scrolls through his emails when he's up at night. If that's the case, I could hear from him any time. If not, I'll get an email first thing in the morning his time."

"Keep us posted," Bobby said.

"Please do," Joe added.

Tess smiled. "So, what are you guys doing today to keep America safe?"

Twenty minutes later as they were wrapping up lunch, Tess glanced at her phone. She giggled.

"Something good?" Jack asked.

"I'll let Bobby do the honors," she said, handing him her phone.

Bobby read the email aloud for the group. "Dear Tess, My sincere apologies for the delay in sending the contract. Yes, the terms you outlined are acceptable. You will have the signed contract by the end of the business day. Thank you for granting us this opportunity. It is our great honor to continue bringing your work to Chinese and Taiwanese audiences. We hold you in the highest esteem and feel fortunate to work with you. My mother is doing as well as she can be.

Thank you for inquiring. The lavender oil you sent helps soothe her. That was very thoughtful. I hope to see you in Taipei again soon. Warm wishes, Tihao." He slid the phone back to Tess. "Damn, you called it."

Tess smiled.

"Well done, baby," Jack said, leaning over to kiss her.

"So Tess, I'll be picking up lunch tomorrow. Any special requests?" Joe asked.

"Thank you, but I won't be here."

"Sweetheart, what are you talking about?" Jack asked, surprised.

She turned to face him. "I have to go to the library to do research for my book. I'm a week behind." She then turned to the group. "You've all been very sweet and it's lovely having lunch with three handsome men, but we all have things to do."

"Well, we'll sure miss having you here," Bobby said. "Come back anytime you want."

Jack grabbed Tess's hand. "I can take the day off and go with you tomorrow."

"Nonsense. You have a job to do. With all the time you're spending with me, I'm seriously beginning to worry about the safety of this country," she said with a giggle. "I don't need a chaperone. I'll be fine."

"We can talk more about this later," he said, concern emanating from every pore.

"We can talk later, but it won't change anything. We all need to get on with life," she replied.

"Jack, let's clean this up and let Tess get back to work," Joe suggested.

Bobby started clearing away the garbage. "Congrats again on your deal, Tess. You're a total boss."

Jack kissed Tess and followed his friends out of the room.

"Relax," Joe said, placing his hand on Jack's shoulder.

They all walked to Jack's office. As soon as he shut the door, he said, "It's too soon," with panic in his eyes.

"For whom, you or Tess?" Joe asked.

Jack stared daggers at him.

"I didn't mean it that way. It's just that she seems okay. I mean, my God, did you hear her on the phone?"

"Joe's right," Bobby added. "She was on fire."

"That's different," Jack said, his face creased with worry.

"You have to let her live her life. Maybe closing that deal was just what she needed to feel like her old self again. If you truly don't think she's ready, talk to her tonight and convince her not to go alone. But this isn't the place for it. You'll just upset her," Joe said.

Jack took a deep breath. "I appreciate everything you've both said and done. You should get back to work."

As soon as they left his office, Jack called Omar.

"Hello?"

"It's Jack. Tess wants to go to the library alone tomorrow."

"I know. She texted me an hour ago."

"I'm worried about her being alone," Jack said.

"I understand, but I think you have to let her do this. We can't treat her like a child. The fact is that she hasn't tried to harm herself, and she seems to be doing remarkably well considering everything that's happened. It's good that she wants to work."

"How do you know she won't slip into a bad state of mind and that something won't happen to her?" Jack asked.

"I don't know. We can never know that with certainty. But she's a highly capable adult and we have to trust her. We need to make sure she will tell us honestly how she's doing and will ask for help if she needs it. That's all we can do."

"I don't like it," Jack said.

"I know it's hard because it's all still fresh, but it will get easier."

"Okay. Thank you."

"Bye."

"Bye."

After hanging up, Jack picked up the framed wedding photo on this desk, held it against his chest, and prayed that Omar was right.

***

When they got home, they made a quick dinner together and ate in front of the TV. The moment they were done, Tess said, "Let's go to bed." She disappeared into their bathroom and reemerged wearing a pink silk slip.

"Wow, what's this?" he asked.

"We haven't been together in a week. We usually can't make it through the day."

He took her hand and looked down. "I know, but…"

"Don't you still want to be with me?" she asked.

He put his hands on her hips. "More than anything. I just don't want to hurt you."

"You can't," she said, and she pulled the slip over her head.

After making love, they lay beside each other, face to face. Jack absentmindedly ran his fingers through her hair.

"Do you feel how much I love you?" he asked.

"Yes."

"Good. Don't forget."

***

When the alarm rang the next morning, they lay in bed a bit longer to hold each other, then got up to brush their teeth. Jack hopped in the shower and Tess returned to the bedroom. When Jack came out, Tess was balled up in a chair in the corner of the room.

He knelt in front of her. "Sweetheart, what's wrong?"

"It's just… I haven't been alone in a week. The last time I was at home by myself…"

He pulled her toward him. "It's okay. It's okay. If it's too soon, I can stay with you or you can come with me."

"I need to be able to do this, so please be supportive. It's just a little harder than I thought. You won't be there with me."

"We can FaceTime all day, any time you want to talk or see me, even if it's every five minutes. And if you want me to come home or to pick you up, just say the word. Promise me you will."

"I promise," she said.

"Hang on." Jack got up and went to put on some music. He selected "All of Me" and then walked over to Tess, extending his hand. "Dance with me, my love."

He put his hand on the small of her back and she leaned against his chest. They swayed to the music, lost in the comfort of their embrace. When the song was over, Jack whispered, "Now you can feel me all day." She smiled and they kissed.

When Jack got into his car, he sat for a long moment to compose himself. He called Tess as soon as he got to his office. She sounded out of breath. "Honey, I'm just finishing my run, can we talk later?"

"Sure," he replied.

An hour and a half later, she FaceTimed him from outside the library.

"Hey, honey. I'm about to go into the library and I just wanted to say hi."

"How are you doing?"

"Fine, I guess. But I miss your face."

"I miss yours, too," he said.

"See you later."

Three hours passed and Jack hadn't heard from Tess. He was wary of being overbearing, so he texted Omar, who had spoken to her an hour earlier. Jack still found it incredibly difficult not to check on her, and he eventually gave in.

She answered his FaceTime call, seated in the library stacks, her glasses askew. She whispered, "Hey, baby. They don't allow cell phone use. You're going to get me in trouble."

"I just wanted to see your pretty face," he said quietly.

She smiled.

"How's it going?" he asked.

"I just read the most fascinating study about how our brains process literature. I'll tell you about it tonight, but for now, I really need to go. I have a lot to get through and the reference librarian is giving me dirty looks."

"Okay, sweetheart. I'll see you tonight. How about I pick up takeout?"

"Sounds great. Love you."

"I love you too," he said.

Jack felt a wave of relief. He was grinning from ear to ear when Joe knocked on his door.

"You look like you just got some good news," Joe said.

"I just FaceTimed with Tess. She's doing research for her book. She seemed good. Really good, actually. Like her old self."

Days passed, each one easier than the last. Tess was immersed in her book project, Jack was back to feeling fully invested at work, they saw their friends every Friday night, and each day they laughed and loved more. They were happy. On the Wednesday exactly six weeks from the day Jack found Tess hiding in the closet, something changed.

CHAPTER 14

This Wednesday morning when the alarm sounded, Tess hopped out of bed before Jack could even say good morning. Knowing her as intimately as he did, he was immediately concerned.

When she emerged from the bathroom, he walked over and put his arms around her waist. "You got out of bed so quickly I couldn't even kiss you good morning," he said.

"Just trying to get a jump-start on the day," she said, slipping out from his arms. "I'll go make coffee."

When Jack was dressed and came into the kitchen, he saw Tess struggling to sort almonds. He watched as she spilled some out on the counter, started counting them, and then pushed them all back together and started again. He approached her from behind and put his hand on her shoulder.

"What are you doing, love?"

"I'm trying to make my snack. You know that Omar makes me bring a snack everywhere, but I keep messing up," she said, her hands trembling.

He placed his hand over hers. "That's okay. I'll do it for you."

"Twelve almonds in each Ziploc. No broken ones, please," she said, stepping to the side.

He prepared the bags and placed the lid on the tub of almonds. "Here you go," he said.

"Thank you."

"Sweetheart, what's wrong?" he asked gently.

"I'm just having a stressful work week."

"Do you promise that's all it is?"

"Yes," she replied.

"I can stay home today if you want. We can hang out."

"Jack, please go to work. I'm fine. I'm gonna jump in the shower."

She tried to sneak past him, but he took her hand. "Hey. Just wait a second, please," he said. He leaned in and kissed her passionately. "I love you."

"Love you too," she said, before walking off.

As soon as he heard the shower turn on, he called Omar.

"Hello," Omar said.

"Hi Omar, it's Jack. Something's up with Tess. She was squirrelly this morning when we got up and then she was shaky and counting her food. She hasn't done that in ages. She said she's just having a stressful work week, but I'm worried."

"She's okay."

"Then you know what's going on with her?" Jack asked.

"She didn't confide in me, but yes, I know what's troubling her. It's nothing like what you're thinking. It truly is work related, and for a normal person it wouldn't be anything bad, quite the contrary. I don't like keeping things from you when you're concerned, but I want to give her the chance to tell you herself."

"Are you sure she's okay?" Jack asked.

"Yes, as much as Tess ever is. We have our usual breakfast tomorrow; I'll try to talk to her."

"Thank you," Jack said.

"I promise that if she doesn't tell you what's going on by Friday night, I'll tell you when we come over for game night."

"Okay. Bye."

"Bye."

Jack called to check on Tess several times that day. He promised to pick up her favorite Indian takeout on the way home. He came home early with the food and a bouquet of white hydrangeas.

"Thank you, baby. They're beautiful," she said.

They sat on the couch eating dinner and watching an old movie. When they went to bed, Jack snuggled up behind her and draped his arm over her. They woke up the next morning exactly as they had fallen asleep.

Tess leapt out of bed and went to brush her teeth. When she opened the bathroom door, Jack was standing outside it. He gave her hand a squeeze. "Wait for me," he said.

He went into the bathroom and when he emerged, he approached Tess and caressed the sides of her body. "I'm enforcing the house codes."

She smiled. He began kissing her. He picked her up and carried her to the bed. After making love, they lay gazing at each other. "I love you with my whole heart, forever," he said.

"I love you, too. You're going to be late. You should get going."

"Okay, baby."

At noon, he called Omar to ask about breakfast with Tess.

"She sent me a text message to cancel," he said.

"I'm really worried," Jack said.

"I promise you she's okay. I know exactly what this is about. I'm still hoping she'll tell you herself, but if not, I'll tell you tomorrow night."

Jack reluctantly agreed.

The next morning, Tess tried to leap out of bed, but Jack stopped her. "Hey, please just stay here with me for a minute."

She lay back down.

"Can I ask you something?" he said.

"Uh huh."

"When you wake up each morning, have you ever thought to yourself, 'Today I can die' or 'Today I can live?'"

"No. I just get up and go on with the day."

He cuddled her and said, "Okay."

"I do think about how grateful I am that you're here."

He smiled.

Later, Jack again found Tess in the kitchen, struggling to sort almonds. Without a word, he gently took over the task.

"Thank you," she said. She looked up at him like she was about to cry.

"What is it, baby? Can't you tell me what's going on?" he asked.

"It's not important. It's just a bad work week. I'll be fine once this week is over. I promise."

"Everyone's supposed to come here tonight for game night, but I can cancel if you want."

"No, don't do that. It'll be nice to hang out with everyone and I already bought tons of food."

"Okay," he said.

"Jack, I really am fine."

He went to work, but he thought about Tess all day. They spoke once at lunchtime, but when he called later in the day, she didn't answer and her voicemail was full.

CHAPTER 15

When Jack got home, Tess was arranging a crudité platter in the kitchen. He noticed two bouquets of flowers at the end of the bar.

"Those are pretty," he said. "Who are they from?"

"My publisher."

"I tried calling you a few times. Did you know that your voicemail is full?"

"Sorry, I turned my ringer off."

"Hey, don't I get a kiss?" he asked.

"I'm sorry, baby. I'm just trying to get everything ready before they get here," she said. She walked over and gave him a quick kiss.

"Joe went on a second date with that artist you set him up with. He's crazy about her, says he owes you big time," Jack said.

Tess smiled. Just then, the timer beeped. "The quiche is ready," she said.

"It smells good. I'm going to go change and then I'll help."

"Great."

As Jack was walking past the flowers, he noticed a card. Tess was preoccupied with the food, so he glanced at it. The card read: "Sometimes good things happen to good people. I'm so happy for you that I could pop. Love, Claire."

***

Everyone was standing around the kitchen making small talk as Tess placed the cheese and charcuterie platter on the bar.

"Where are Omar and Clay?" Joe asked.

"I guess they're running late," Tess said. "Maybe they got held up at work."

"The traffic was bad," Bobby said, taking a swig of his beer.

The doorbell rang. Jack hit the buzzer and opened the door for Omar and Clay, whose hands were full.

"Sorry, we're late," Omar said, flitting inside, holding a jumbo pink cardboard cake box. Clay followed behind with a brown paper bag under one arm and a vase of white flowers in the other. "We had to stop to pick up celebratory supplies," Omar said, kissing Tess on the forehead and placing the large pastry box on the counter. "We have the most wonderful cake."

"And I have lots of champagne, and of course, a bottle of the best sparkling water for you, Tess," Clay added. "These are for you," Clay said, handing Tess the flowers.

Tess smiled sheepishly and placed them on the bar in front of her. She looked at Omar. "Who told you?"

"Crystal," he said, taking off his coat and handing it to Clay.

"She's fired," Tess replied.

"No, she's not," Omar said. "Besides, the press release went out yesterday. The whole literary world knows, Butterfly."

"There was a press release?" Tess groaned.

Omar rolled his eyes. "Of course. You know how these things work."

Tess was silent as everyone in the room stared at her.

Omar looked around. "Hmm, two bouquets. I know of at least thirty people who asked for your address. I'm guessing you had deliveries all day."

Tess looked down. "I had them picked up and taken to a local hospital. Those came after the pick-up."

"Uh huh, hiding the evidence, I see," Omar said. "Not the sign of well-being."

"Oh hush," Tess said.

Jack looked at Tess and Omar. "What are we celebrating?"

"Oh, sweet Butterfly, you haven't even told Jack? Just when I thought you were getting close to sanity," Omar said, kissing her forehead again.

"Perish the thought," Tess whispered. She looked up, everyone's eyes on her. She focused on Jack. "It's nothing," she said. "It's not a big deal."

"If by 'not a big deal' you mean 'a hugely big deal,' then you'd be right," Omar said. "You see, our very own brilliant Tess has won the highly coveted American Novel Award for her last book."

Jack grinned from ear to ear. "That's so great!"

"Wow, congratulations!" Joe exclaimed.

Everyone chimed in with congratulatory words.

"That's not all," Omar said. "For mere mortals, this would be an incredible achievement, but Tess is anything but ordinary. It's a historic win."

"The word historic is really overused," Tess protested. "Just because something hasn't happened before doesn't mean it's historic."

"Uh, actually, that's literally what it means," Omar said.

"I have to side with him on that one," Bobby said.

Tess rolled her eyes.

"Tess has won this award before," Omar said. "She's the first author to ever win twice. And she was the youngest recipient, so actually, she's made history twice."

Tess gave him the side eye.

Jack was beaming. "That's amazing," he said, wrapping her in a hug.

"Wow, Tess. That's a truly incredible achievement," Joe said.

"We're so happy for you," Bobby added.

Tess looked down, seemingly embarrassed by the attention. She smiled half-heartedly. "Thanks," she mumbled. "I'll go get the cake plates from the china cabinet." She headed toward the dining room.

Joe furrowed his brow. "What's going on?"

Everyone leaned in. Omar quietly said, "We are going to celebrate this. It must be celebrated. When she comes back, please go sit down in the living room and talk about her writing and books. She likes talking about those things. Just don't mention the award. Jack, stay behind with me for a minute."

Tess shuffled back in and held her hands up to show the cake plates. "I'll put these in there," she said quietly, heading into the living room. "Jack, can you bring some forks, please?"

"Sure, sweetheart."

"Jack and I will pour the bubbly. Be there in a flash," Omar added.

Everyone followed Tess into the living room, except for Omar and Jack.

Jack waved Omar to the far side of the kitchen and quietly said, "Listen, I appreciate what you're trying to do, but she's been off for days."

"That's because she has no ability to embrace her success. I've been watching this same cycle for over fifteen years. It ends tonight. This is a massive achievement and she deserves to enjoy it."

"I know how much you care about her, but she's been happy until this week. I can't forget that it was only six weeks ago that… that I was afraid of losing her. Do you remember how fragile and dissociated she was? I don't think we should push her."

"Jack, I know how protective you are. I would lay down my own life before I would hurt her. I believe we can help her. I know we can. I need you to trust me. Please."

Jack inhaled deeply.

"She deserves every happiness in this life," Omar said.

"What do you need me to do?" Jack asked.

"Just be there with her, supportively. She feels the most comfortable with you around. I'll take care of everything else."

Jack nodded. "Promise you'll shut it down if it's too much."

"Of course," Omar said. "And Jack, if I'm able to get her there, whatever you say or do, no matter how small, it will matter more than anything else. That's what she'll remember."

"Where are you guys?" Tess called.

"Just getting the drinks, sweetheart," Jack replied.

***

Tess sat on the far side of the couch. Jack sat beside her with Bobby to his left. Joe, Gina, and Clay were seated in chairs around the coffee table. After handing everyone their champagne flutes, Omar sat in the recliner adjacent to Tess.

"So, let's have a toast," Omar said, raising his glass.

Tess raised her glass. "To friendship," she said, before anyone else had a chance to speak.

"Oh, Butterfly," Omar said, shaking his head. "To friendship."

"To friendship," everyone chimed in.

Tess took a sip of her sparkling water and set her glass on the coffee table.

Joe said, "Tess, you never finished what you were going to say." He turned to Jack and Omar. "Tess was just about to tell us if she has a favorite line from any of her books."

"Over the years, I felt like I revealed so much of myself in my novels, so the one thing I kept private is what they each mean to me. I felt like it was the only thing I had left that was mine. The things that mean the most to me are innocuous; they are nothing that would stand out to anyone else. There are a few lines that readers constantly bring up, but I never share my favorite. But I'll tell you."

"You know anything you tell us stays in this room," Bobby said.

"Absolutely," Joe added.

"I bet I know," Omar said. "They are your favorite words, after all."

Tess smiled. "Yeah."

Omar continued. "The female character says, 'Do you remember?' and the male character says, 'I remember.' It's so simple, but I know that's your favorite bit."

Tess nodded. "It's hard to explain. I guess I think there's nothing more affirming than a shared memory. To me, it's like someone saying, 'You exist and I see you.' That's all people really want."

"I loved that book," Gina said. "I did notice that part. Hearing what it means to you makes me realize that I was right to think those were special words."

Tess smiled.

Omar leaned forward in his chair. "Tess, we so badly want to celebrate this achievement with you."

She sighed.

"I know you think awards are ridiculous," Omar said.

"Because they are," she quipped back.

"And I know you think humility is a virtue," he said.

"Because it is," she replied.

"But I've never believed those are the reasons you can't seem to find any happiness in your success. I know you think I'm torturing you," Omar said.

"Because you are," she replied.

"Just tell us why. I've watched for so many years and it's like every kind word or bit of recognition hurts you, like it physically hurts you. Please tell us why."

"The people's high priestess of pain is crowned again. I just want the coronation to end."

"Oh, Butterfly."

"Okay, I'll tell you," she said softly, curling her legs up on the couch. "When my first novel came out, I was inundated with emails and letters from readers telling me how they connected to the book. They would tell me their stories – all kinds of horrible traumas, abuse, self-hatred, self-harm, depression, all manner of suffering. At book signings, people would wait in line for hours just to whisper their stories to me. It's been like that ever since with each book. You see, books do well when they resonate. They sell. The success of my books reflects only one thing: how many people are in pain. I just don't know how to celebrate that."

"Is that really how you see it?" Omar asked.

"Yes," Tess whispered.

"Oh, sweet Butterfly, don't you understand what inspirational means? That's what they call your books."

"Tess," Gina said. "You know I'm a huge fan of your work, but I never told you this when we met because I didn't want to make you uncomfortable. For years, I was in one toxic relationship after another. The guy I was with before Bobby liked to use me as a punching bag. I read *Candy Floss* for strength. When I finished reading it, I decided to change my life. With the courage I found in your words, I walked out and never looked back. I honestly don't think I'd be here without it. I've read it so many times that the pages are falling out. Yes, it resonated with me because I was in pain, but it also saved me."

"It's true," Bobby said. "She wanted to tell you ages ago."

Tess smiled faintly.

Joe chimed in. "I read *The Island* about five or six years ago. I was going through a tough time. We see so much horror in our line of work. It helped restore my faith in humanity. Truly, it did. There was no rosy version of reality. It was gritty but hopeful. I needed that more than I knew at the time. Pain and suffering are inevitable in this world. Your books don't cause the pain or celebrate it – they offer respite."

"Thanks, guys," Tess muttered. "I appreciate it. I do."

"You know what I think we need? Cake," Omar said, leaping up.

Tess leaned on Jack. He embraced her, rubbing her arm.

"When he ordered this cake, he said it was the happiest he had ever been to buy something," Clay said.

"He's very sweet," Tess said. Then she whispered to Jack, "I don't eat cake."

"We can share a piece," he whispered, kissing the top of her head.

"Shut your eyes, Tess," Omar hollered.

Tess obliged. When she opened them, there was a large round cake in the center of the table. In gold script, it said, "Congratulations, Tess! We love you!" Dozens of gold and silver shooting stars surrounded the lettering and borders of the cake.

Tess gasped. She leaned forward. Her eyes flooded with hot tears. "It's wonderful. I can't believe you remembered," she said.

"How could I ever forget?" Omar replied.

"That's the only time I ever shared that story with anyone," she said, happy tears streaming down her face.

"I assumed," he replied.

She wiped her cheeks and looked up at the group. "It was years ago. We were in Chicago. I had been on the road for months doing book talks and signings. I was doing a bunch of stops in Illinois, and when I was in Urbana-Champaign, I caught a terrible cold. I was mostly upset because I had been looking forward to meeting Omar in Chicago." She turned to Jack. "Remember, we told you about that night."

He nodded.

"Anyway, we hadn't seen each other in months and we were meant to have fun together, but by then I was too sick. So, he stayed with me in my suite at the Westin. We ordered loads of room service and watched *Moulin Rouge* for the billionth time. I was on so much cold medicine and I was hugely grumpy."

"She was," Omar interjected with a smile. "God, she's an awful patient."

Tess giggled. "So, to try to cheer me up, he acted out each dance number."

"Smashingly, I might add," Omar said.

Tess smiled. "You were marvelous, such flair. And it did cheer me up. After the movie ended and we were done gorging ourselves, we lay in bed talking. There's a scene in the movie where Satine sings a song called, 'Someday I'll Fly Away.' It's the most subtle number in the film, but it was so powerful. She sings about how she's dreamt of flying away her whole life, but she wonders if it's worth it to dream because of what might happen when the dreams end." She turned to face Omar. "You've always wanted to know why I love that movie so much; it's that song." She turned back to the group. "I was thinking about that song and that's when I told him." She stopped to take a breath. "You all know what my childhood was like."

They nodded.

"I didn't believe in God, so I didn't have anything to pray to for help. One day, my aunt gave me a packet of those glow-in-the-dark shooting star stickers. She said if you make a wish on a shooting star it comes true. So I stuck the stickers on the ceiling above my bed, and every night I wished on them over and over and over again. No matter how tired I was, I forced myself to stay awake as long as I possibly could to keep wishing. I always wished for the same thing. I made that wish for years," she said, wiping another tear from her eyes.

Jack rubbed her arm.

"Eventually, I stopped believing. The day I moved out of that horrible house, I had two clear thoughts: I wanted to write so that I could give people something to believe in, even if I didn't; and I never wanted to see another shooting star again. I couldn't bear to live in a world where you can wish thousands of times and your wish never comes true."

"I thought it was safe now," Omar said. "You never said what your single wish was, but I believe I know. And I believe it has come true."

"It has," she whispered.

"What was your wish?" Jack asked softly.

She looked at him. "This. I wished for exactly what I have, with all of you" she said, looking at the faces of her beloved friends, "and especially you," she said, turning to Jack and squeezing his hand.

"Tess," Omar said.

She turned to face him.

"You have spent your entire adult life turning darkness into light. In doing so, you've helped countless people, including the ones in this room. That is why your readers love you and that is why you've received recognition for your work. That is what this award honors: transforming darkness into light. And *that* is something that ought to be celebrated."

She sniffled, took a breath, and said, "Okay. I can celebrate that."

Omar smiled. "Come here," he said, rising.

She stood up and hugged him tightly. "Thank you."

"I'm so happy for you. You're brilliant and you deserve this."

"Thank you," she whispered again.

"And you will always have two men who love you," he said.

When they separated, she wiped her face and said, "Well, I guess someone should cut the cake."

"That's my job," Clay said, picking up the knife.

As he was passing out pieces of cake, Tess sat down and leaned against Jack. "I'm so proud of you," he whispered.

She smiled.

"Are you two sharing?" Clay asked, his arm outstretched with a plate.

"I'll have my own," Tess said. "Just a small piece, please."

***

"Now that we've had dessert, everyone help yourselves to some food," Tess said, gesturing toward the kitchen. "Are you coming?" she asked Jack as she started to get up.

"I'll be right there. Omar and I will clean up the cake plates."

Clay carried the leftover cake and everyone headed into the kitchen. Jack approached Omar. "Thank you for what you did for Tess. She's lucky to have you. I couldn't have done that."

Omar smiled. "It wouldn't have been possible without you. Any happiness she has now is because of you."

Jack put his arm on Omar's shoulder, leaned in to hug him, and said, "We're family."

They collected the plates and joined the others. Tess was serving Gina a slice of quiche when the doorbell rang.

"I'll get it," Jack said. He returned a moment later with a vase of red roses. "Sweetheart, you got a flower delivery."

She smiled. "That's nice."

Jack looked at the card. "Uh, do you have a friend named Bruce?"

"I have two friends named Bruce," she replied. "Gina, you would love this guy I know; he's an elementary school art teacher and he does the most amazing puppet-making project with his kids."

"Sweetheart, is your other friend a musician, by chance?" Jack asked.

"Yup," she said, serving Joe some quiche.

"I think this is from him," Jack said, placing the vase on the counter. "Do you want to see the card?"

"Can you read it?" she asked.

"Blinded by the light always. Well done. Love, Bruce."

"Oh, that's sweet," Tess said.

Bobby's jaw dropped. "You know Jack loves his music."

"Oh, well you should meet him sometime. Great guy. Bobby, would you like some quiche?"

They filled their plates and returned to the living room.

After tasting the eggplant dip, Omar said, "Butterfly, this is delicious. Is it Layla's recipe? You know how I love it."

Tess nodded and jumped up. "I should probably give Bruce a quick call to thank him for the flowers."

As soon as she left the room, Gina asked, "Why do you call her Butterfly?"

Jack looked up from his plate. "I asked her once after we first met, but she said she didn't know. I've always wondered."

Omar laughed. "I've been calling her that since her first book came out. She never asked why. She just accepted it."

"Is it because butterflies are so beautiful?" Gina asked.

"Metamorphosis?" Joe asked.

Jack shook his head. "I think it's the butterfly effect."

Omar smiled. "Yes, you're on to it. The butterfly effect essentially says that something as small as a butterfly flapping her wings can change the entire world. I've always found it to contain a paradox: tragedy and beauty. The butterfly will never understand how the flap of her wings has changed the world, and therein is her tragedy. But because she can never understand her impact, she has only the moment, the very movement of her wings, and so she is always fully present in the now. And therein is her beauty."

Jack smiled.

Tess returned and plopped back down on the couch.

"How's Bruce?" Omar asked.

"Good. He's writing a new song. The lyrics are wonderful. So you all co-opted this evening, but it's still a game night. What are we playing?"

"That's my Butterfly," Omar said.

***

Tess and Jack were nestled together on the couch. "No one wanted to play Jenga with you since you've diffused bombs and all, but after your colossal loss, I'm a little concerned that the country isn't as safe as I thought," Tess teased.

"You distracted me," Jack protested.

"I did nothing of the sort. I feel a little guilty we're not helping clean up. You guys are spoiling us," she called.

"You can't do the dishes at your own celebration," Omar replied.

"We'll have this place spotless in no time," Joe said.

"Make sure you all take some of the leftover food and cake," Tess hollered.

"I'm on it," Clay called.

Jack ran his fingers through Tess's hair. "We have the best friends," she said.

"Yeah, we do," he said. "You know, Omar finally told us why he calls you Butterfly. Do you want to know?"

"Not really."

He chuckled. "He would have guessed as much." He squeezed her hand and said, "I'm so proud of you. Have I told you that?"

"Uh huh."

"It's a big weekend. What should we do to celebrate?" he asked.

"Normal stuff. Let's go to a movie, or watch a game, or take a walk. I just want to be together."

He pulled her chin to him and gently pressed his lips to hers. "Okay."

She nuzzled into him and looked up at the mantel covered in framed photos of the two of them, her and Omar, Gracie, and all their friends. "Jack, do you remember the first night we met when I said that reality never lives up to our dreams?"

"I remember."

"Perhaps it's our dreams that can never capture all that is actually possible."

EPILOGUE

Four Months Later

"We're deeply honored to have you back at New York University, Ms. Lee. There's been so much excitement for your visit that you'll see the auditorium is completely packed, standing room only."

Tess smiled, holding Jack's hand as their host guided them backstage. They passed a custodian who glanced at Tess and looked down. She walked over and shook his hand. Once they reached the backstage wing, her host said, "There's water on stage for you. Are you sure I can't get you anything else?"

"I'm fine, thank you."

"After I introduce you, I thought we could spend half an hour having a conversation, and then open it up for audience questions for the last fifteen minutes before the book signing."

"Sure," Tess replied.

"How long would you like to stay at the signing?" he asked.

"Until everyone's had their books signed," she replied.

Jack smiled.

"Wonderful," her host replied. "A few of us were planning to take you to The Odeon in Tribeca afterward for lunch. I remembered you liked it there."

"Perfect. Thank you."

"Well, this is it. I'm going to introduce you."

He walked on stage and Tess stayed with Jack.

"Welcome to this very special event. There's so much I could say about Tess Lee. I would love to list her books, her awards, and share some of the things that have been written about her over the years, but she asked me not to do any of that."

The audience laughed.

"I suppose it doesn't matter; you're all gathered here because you already know those things. Instead, I will just share what today means to me. Tess Lee's books have brought me comfort, hope, and strength. On dark days, they have been the words in my head, reminding me that there is light at the end of the tunnel. When Ms. Lee accepted the invitation to speak here today, I was overcome. Then, she called me herself to tell me how much she was looking forward to it. Yeah, I did a happy dance in my office. So, it is my great honor to introduce author Tess Lee."

Jack kissed Tess. "Knock 'em dead, Mrs. Miller."

Tess walked onstage to a standing ovation.

After their conversation about the power of literature, the host invited questions from the audience. The Q&A went smoothly and quickly, and before long, there was only time for one final question. A woman stood up and said, "Your characters are always fighting personal battles, many related to past traumas, but your books have hopeful messages. Do you believe that healing is possible?"

"I don't think I'm any better equipped to answer that than anyone else in this room, but I will share this from my own experience. When I was in high school, I had a boyfriend who wanted to get married. I didn't feel that way about him and ended the relationship. He told me, 'No one will ever be able to fill the hole in your soul.' I still remember those words like it happened yesterday. He was hurt and he wanted to hurt me in return. For a long time, those words haunted me like a shadow. Eventually, I realized that we're lucky if we end up with a hole in our soul. You see, our wounds don't start out that way. They're jagged. They have rough edges. They are like flesh that has been ripped from our body. If we learn to let love into our lives, over time, the jagged edges become smooth, and only a hole remains. Sometimes that love comes from a friend's laughter, the hug of a child, or the embrace of a lover who sees who we really are. Sometimes giving love freely and with your whole heart can heal you, too. When there aren't people to provide that love, it can come from a song, or a movie, or even a novel. And that is why I write."

SUGGESTED CLASSROOM OR BOOK CLUB USE

1. What do you think about Tess and Jack's relationship? What is special about their relationship, and why is their bond so strong? What role does past trauma play in their love story and how they choose to treat one another?

2. The friendship between Tess and Omar is the other primary "love" story in this novel. What do you think about their relationship? What does this relationship say about the families we choose to create? Can you draw comparisons between this friendship and any of your own?

3. How do the characters communicate with each other? Consider the verbal and physical aspects of their communication. What do their patterns of interaction reveal about their relationships?

4. *Shooting Stars* suggests that love, in its many forms, can help us heal. Explore this theme in relation to any of the main or supporting characters. What about with yourself or your loved ones?

5. The issue of coping with sexual abuse and trauma is central to the story. What do we learn from Tess's experience? What can we learn from the ways Omar and Jack help her?

6. Grief is central to Jack's story. What can we learn from his experience with Gracie? How does Tess help him?

7. Issues related to privilege surface throughout the book, for example, in mentions of homelessness, racism, and sexism. Explore this topic using examples from the book and what you think about the characters and their perspectives.

8. Popular culture is filled with examples of toxic masculinity. While negative male forces lurk in the shadows of *Shooting Stars* (e.g., Arlo, Chris, Tess's abusers, Tess's father), the primary characters exhibit positive masculinity. Discuss this in relation to any of the characters (Jack, Joe, Bobby, Omar, and/or Clay).

9. Themes of darkness and light appear repeatedly in *Shooting Stars*. What are some examples? What's the purpose of this theme?

10. *Shooting Stars* is a book about love. What is the overall message about love? Find some examples that support your contention.

CREATIVE WRITING ACTIVITIES

1. Bobby, Joe, Gina, and Clay are supporting characters. Select one of these characters and write their story.
2. Select one of the characters and look ahead five years. Write a short story based on where you think they end up.
3. If *Shooting Stars* was a play instead of a novel, it would likely include monologues by the main characters. Select a character and write their pivotal monologue.
4. In Chapter 5, Tess recites "the cereal scene" from her latest novel. Use this scene or imagine a different part of the novel to write an original short story.
5. Write an alternative ending to *Shooting Stars*.

QUALITATIVE RESEARCH ACTIVITIES

1. Select several scenes and perform discourse or conversation analysis on the dialogue. For example, use one of the conversations at Shelby's Bar, a conversation between Tess and Jack, or any other exchange.
2. Research sexual assault and locate peer-reviewed articles or scholarly essays on related issues (e.g., rape culture, family abuse, gender and violence, trauma). Use your findings to write a paper, using Tess's experiences to illustrate or challenge your research.

ART ACTIVITIES

1. Create a visual or audiovisual version of "the cereal scene" that Tess recites from her novel.
2. Respond artistically to *Shooting Stars*. Using any medium – literary, visual, or performative – create an artistic response to a theme in the novel or express how the novel made you feel.

AUTHOR Q&A

What inspired this novel?

I've always wanted to write a love story. When I was about ten years old, I began to give serious thought to becoming a writer. I tried writing a novel at the time, an epic love story between people who help each other heal, but because I was ten, it didn't pan out. By the time I became a professional author, I had long since abandoned the idea of writing about love. Then one day, *Shooting Stars* came to me in a burst, which was very different from the way my other novels have materialized. Usually, I stew on an idea for a while, and then spend a year or two drafting a manuscript. *Shooting Stars* came to me quickly, and I wrote the entire first draft in about ten days. I barely slept, I didn't respond to emails, and if anyone spoke to me, I'm sure I didn't hear a word they said. I was completely immersed, more than I'd been with anything before.

What was the writing process like?

I spent every waking moment of every day and night mentally in this story's world. It was an immersive, emotional, and cathartic experience. I've never enjoyed writing anything more than *Shooting Stars*. The writing process was completely different than my previous novels. Typically, I draft a rough outline and then write the novel in chronological order. I viewed this one as a compilation of scenes, and that's how I wrote it – completely out of order. In fact, the last chapter in the book was the first one I wrote, then I skipped around in the middle, and I finished by writing the first chapter. I also didn't utilize some of the literary devices I've used in the past. There's no interior monologue, nor are there any flashbacks. I wanted readers to experience these characters as they experience each other: together and in real time, through their interactions and dialogue. The structure of this novel is also completely organic; there was no formula.

How do you see Tess and Jack?

I think they have a beautiful relationship. There's a saying that, "Hurt people hurt people," but that's not always the case. Sometimes, people in deep pain are able to love others in extraordinary ways, without widening the circle of trauma.

What do you hope readers take away from this book?

Love is possible. Healing is possible. Healing is possible if we let love into our lives, whether that love comes from friends who understand us, lovers who truly see us, or the art we make or experience, like a song, a movie, or even a novel. We need to be gentle with one another, just as the friends and lovers in this novel are.

How would you describe Shooting Stars?

It's a love letter to love.

Will you write more books about Tess and Jack?

Yes. Sometimes, when I complete a novel, I feel like I can say goodbye to the characters and imagine them as I left them. Other times, I know the next chapter, and that was the case with this book. I've already written four more volumes, all of which I love as much as the original. I'm not sure when we'll release them. Stay tuned! Each Tess Lee and Jack Miller novel explores love at the intersection of another theme; in *Shooting Stars* the theme I explore is love and healing. By the fourth novel, the characters will come full circle. By the fifth novel, the characters will fully move forward in new ways.

ABOUT THE AUTHOR

Patricia Leavy, Ph.D., is an independent scholar and bestselling author. She was formerly Associate Professor of Sociology, Chair of Sociology & Criminology, and Founding Director of Gender Studies at Stonehill College in Massachusetts. She has published over thirty books, earning commercial and critical success in both nonfiction and fiction, and her work has been translated into numerous languages. Her recent titles include *The Oxford Handbook of Methods for Public Scholarship*; *Handbook of Arts-Based Research*; *Research Design: Quantitative, Qualitative, Mixed Methods, Arts-Based, and Community-Based Participatory Research Approaches*; *Method Meets Art: Arts-Based Research Practice, Third Edition*; *Fiction as Research Practice*; *The Oxford Handbook of Qualitative Research, Second Edition*; and the novels *Spark*, *Film*, *Blue*, *American Circumstance,* and *Low-Fat Love*. She is also series creator and editor for ten book series with Oxford University Press, Brill | Sense, and Guilford Press, and is cofounder and co-editor-in-chief of *Art/Research International: A Transdisciplinary Journal*. A vocal advocate for public scholarship, she has blogged for numerous outlets, and is frequently called on by the US national news media. In addition to receiving numerous honors for her books, including American Fiction Awards and a Living Now Book Award, she has received career awards from the New England Sociological Association, the American Creativity Association, the American Educational Research Association, the International Congress of Qualitative Inquiry, and the National Art Education Association. In 2016, Mogul, a global women's empowerment network, named her an "Influencer." In 2018, the National Women's Hall of Fame honored her, and SUNY-New Paltz established the "Patricia Leavy Award for Art and Social Justice." Please visit www.patricialeavy.com for more information or for links to her social media.

Made in the USA
Las Vegas, NV
04 February 2021